Through
WOODS & WATERS

A SOLO JOURNEY TO MAINE'S NEW NATIONAL MONUMENT

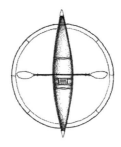

LAURIE APGAR CHANDLER

Through Woods & Waters: A Solo Journey to Maine's New National Monument
Copyright © 2020 Laurie Apgar Chandler

ISBN: 978-1-63381-231-4

Library of Congress Control Number: 2020914508

The following have generously granted permission to quote from copyrighted works. Excerpts from *Tell Me About the River* by Ted Clapp, *Allagash* by Gil Gilpatrick, *Chimney Pond Tales* by Clayton Hall and Jane Thomas with Elizabeth Hall Harmon, *Maine Geographic Canoeing Volume 3: Northern Rivers* by Zip Kellogg, *Katahdin Comrades: The Journals of Lester F. Hall* by Charlotte Hall Kirkpatrick, *Katahdin: An Historic Journey* by John W. Neff, *Maine Sporting Camps* by George Smith, and *The Call of Katahdin* by Ed Werler, courtesy of the authors or their families. Material from *The Wildest Country: Exploring Thoreau's Maine* by J. Parker Huber (Appalachian Mountain Club Books, 2008) used with permission of the publisher.

Cover photograph, "Upper Haskell Rock Pitch, East Branch of the Penobscot River," by Laurie Apgar Chandler

Illustrations by Arnold J. Aho, A.I.A., © 2020

Cover and book design by Wendy Higgins

Designed and produced by:
Maine Authors Publishing
12 High Street, Thomaston, Maine
www.maineauthorspublishing.com

Printed in the United States of America

For all those who give the gifts of woods and waters

And for Arne, who understood the vision

CONTENTS

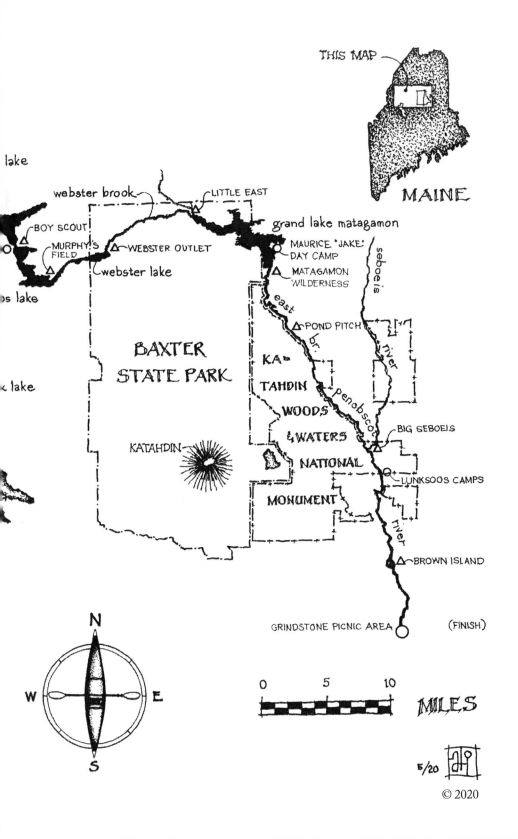

PROLOGUE

*Climb the mountains and get their good tidings. Nature's
peace will flow into you as sunshine flows into trees. The
winds will blow their own freshness into you, and the storms
their energy, while cares will drop off like autumn leaves.*

—**John Muir,** *Our National Parks*

Not far from the Canadian border, in western Maine, the Moose
River flows calmly eastward for eight quiet miles from the town
of Jackman into Long Pond. In the summer of 2012, I was paddling
there for the second time. The year before, I had solo kayaked across
the state of Maine as a fundraiser for the Maine Children's Cancer
Program. Now I was back, on a shorter trip, just for fun.

The weather was changeable that day, in the way that it often
is on northern lakes. Above and to the east, the sky was a brilliant
blue behind pillows of billowing white. To the west, it was a different story. Banks of dark, angry rain clouds were quickly bearing
down. Soon they would envelop my small kayak, a racing yellow dot
on the open water. I was not going to make it to the campsite before the storm.

Ahead, I spotted a small beach. I sprinted in, grabbing the one
bag not under the spray skirts and scooting under the shelter of a
white cedar tree just as the skies opened.

That cedar tree became my haven. The trunk curved slightly inward, protecting me from the full force of the rain. My world was re-

1

duced to the circumference of its spreading branches. I studied the flat, primeval leaves and shaggy, creviced bark, thinking with awe how similar was the white cedar to its Jurassic ancestors. Just beyond, the world disappeared behind a watery curtain.

I leaned my forehead against the trunk, feeling its rough texture, and shut my eyes. Surrendering to the rain, accepting the delay, absorbing the feeling of peace. Wilderness journeys are made by embracing moments such as these. I could almost have dozed, standing there in the warm rain.

Later, I opened my eyes to search for any brightening in the skies. A flash of movement from the sandy, watery blur of the beach became a red fox. Quickly, he darted through the clearing, close and vivid, his russet coat a bright spot of color. Then he was gone, into the trees. Just a moment, a breath, that was almost a dream and, at the same time, forever engraved in my memory.

Gifts of nature are like that. They come when they come, often unlooked-for, and we treasure them even more for their serendipity. As the years have gone by, these are the gifts I have sought out.

At high noon on the day of the summer solstice, many years ago, some small sound halted me along a hiking trail on the south ridge of a Shenandoah mountain. I slowly turned to look. There, among tall grasses, a bobcat and I locked eyes for a long, enduring moment. Crossing a Maine lake one dull gray morning, a tiny hole opened in the solid leaden sky and a single ray of sunshine beamed down like a message from above. These are the moments that bring me joy and give me purpose.

Faith, family, and friends still guide and center me as they have always done, but I have a new passion, to wander alone in wild places and to write. Like a benediction, a rebirth, the written word has opened new avenues for me, at the very time when the roles that I'd had for so long—like motherhood—were changing.

I came to this obsession for long solo trips gradually and perhaps inevitably. Growing up in an outdoorsy family and personally inclined toward natural solitude, I had the camping-alone-in-the-dark piece covered. After moving to Maine with my children in 2003, I met my husband, Chris, who took me to the Allagash Wilderness Waterway for our honeymoon. I fell in love all over again, with the misty dance of the morning river, the heady scent of firs, and the spirit that enriched the wild beauty of its forests.

I lost Chris in 2009. By then, I owned a solo kayak. I began taking longer and longer trips alone, going places we'd dreamed of and journaling. It wasn't long before I had a more ambitious goal, to thru-paddle—like a thru-hike but mainly on the water—the Northern Forest Canoe Trail.

Once more, I turned to the support team that has been there for me all my life, my parents. In 2014, with my children grown and gone, I sold my house and accepted Mom and Dad's generous offer to share their home, moving into their basement bedroom, complete with a woodstove and brand-new bathroom. As they had during my fundraising paddle, they would keep me resupplied, testing the mettle of their truck on some dubious roads, meeting me with food, supplies, and even freshly laundered clothes. Most of all, they would believe in me and trust that all would be well.

The NFCT follows historic waterways for 740 miles, from the Adirondacks to far northern Maine. In late June 2015, I left Old Forge, New York, in a new boat, a 13-foot Wenonah Fusion Kevlar canoe, light enough for the many miles of carries and upstream travel ahead. Fifty-three days later, I paddled gratefully into Fort Kent, Maine, having gone the distance under my own power. The blessings of that adventure were many—friendly weather, caring trail angels, weeks of connecting with both nature and myself, and the affirmation that I was doing what I must.

Coming home was hard. If there were tears when my honeymoon ended, there was a deeper grief now. Thankfully, I had my writing. I'd filled two waterproof journals, which became the foundation for my first book, *Upwards: The Story of the First Woman to Solo Thru-Paddle the Northern Forest Canoe Trail.* I spent the summer of 2017 immersed in editing and design, press proofs and printing. The book was published that fall, and I found I liked the author life, too.

By the spring of 2018, though, I was growing restless to return. When you have traveled far in the northern forest, known its rhythms and become part of them for a time, the woods and waters call you back. To places where human voices hush and nature speaks. Such places find their way into your heart, and you are never truly gone.

Slip away for an hour to walk a forest path or sit along a shore, quiet and listening, and you are home.

Sadly, in our busy lives, such quiet hours must be dearly won. So often, we surrender our true inner selves to the relentless pressures of civilization. My soul longed for the peace, simplicity, and autonomy of a long expedition. To face once again the unknown, with trust and faith, and rediscover the strength and creativity to find my way.

That summer, I decided, I would craft my own route, with challenges reminiscent of the Northern Forest Canoe Trail. I would follow the Wabanaki people, and Thoreau, and countless others whose names I did not know, but whose spirits would flow with mine. There would be plenty of whitewater, old-fashioned carries, and wild weather in wild places. Darkness or circumstances might force me to stealth camp, which, in truth, I greatly enjoy.

After considerable reflection, a route began to emerge. I planned to backpack, as well as travel by canoe. I knew I wanted to write another book. My destination, I hoped, would inspire readers, introducing them to one of Maine's newest natural treasures—a place of untamed rivers, mountain vistas, and rich history. In the telling of my tale, I would strive to weave the threads of discovery, place, and connection into the physical journey forward. The departure date for the backpacking segment was set for July 8, 2018. After returning home briefly to fulfill an author commitment, I would take to my canoe for the remainder of the expedition, with one resupply midway along the paddling route.

Through Woods & Waters does not unfold chronologically. Now and again, as writers know, a story will begin to tell itself with surprising authority. So it was with this one. A chance encounter along a wild river changed the warp and weft of my weaving and encouraged me to start my tale, not at the beginning, but in the middle. Thus, the book has three parts. Part I follows the first half of the canoe route, Part II the backpacking, and Part III the second half of the canoe route, to journey's end.

In the long summer days before my trip, I dreamed of roaming the woods and waters. I wouldn't hurry but would take the days as they came, giving myself permission to camp early or sit for an hour watching a heron. Thoughts that forever danced at the edges of my consciousness would be freed to be explored. I would feel again that deep weariness of muscle and lightness of spirit that comes after many hours of exertion. Most importantly, there were memories to be made. I would be going home.

PART I

THE CANOE TRIP

CHAPTER 1

DROPPING IN

Believe you can and you're halfway there.

—Theodore Roosevelt

Beyond the wide window, a blanket of fog wrapped the rustic lodge in soft folds, revealing just a few clumps of white-skinned birch. Bathed in tiny droplets, the patterns of bark and emerald leaves stood out with an ephemeral beauty that would be gone with the sun. The hour was early, the day newborn.

Inside the lodge, however, my thoughts had drifted far from the peaceful view. Instead, I stared with dreadful fascination at the image on my laptop. Amid churning whiteness, beneath the jagged ledges of a formidable Class III+ drop, was a kayak. A hint of red and the tensed outline of a paddler battled through a cloud of spray, below a brow of unforgiving rock.

Unconsciously, my mind substituted a slight woman, strong and determined, but still a novice at serious whitewater. She was alone, without companions, in a small open canoe made of lightweight Kevlar. Despite hundreds of miles of wilderness paddling experience, she was in no way equipped for drops like this. To attempt to run this rapid would be insane.

The photo was labeled "E-Ledge." A ledge resembles a submerged step extending roughly perpendicular across the river. The higher the step, the more dramatic the drop. In the river description, E-Ledge was preceded by ledges A through D and followed by ledges F through K. Counting on my fingers, that made eleven ledge drops, plus an extra set at the start, labeled "Put-in Ledges." A total of twelve difficult challenges in just the first few miles on the river. The four worst, rated Class III or III+ on American Whitewater's International Scale of River Difficulty, would be characterized by irregular waves, strong eddies, and powerful current that could swamp an open canoe.

How had I missed this?

For months, I'd been devouring trip descriptions, gathering maps and articles, and piecing together the quilt of a journey from the knowledge of those who had gone before. Stumbling across a trip description was like sitting around an imaginary campfire for an evening of storytelling. Bit by bit, the puzzle came together. Tucked away in my dry bags and resupply boxes were well-organized notes meant to guide me over the miles that lay ahead. Now, it was obvious that my research on this part of Maine's West Branch of the Penobscot River had been woefully inadequate.

A few minutes before, I'd come quietly downstairs to the lodge's great room, with my books and maps, an hour before the first hope of coffee. I couldn't sleep, despite the exhausting scramble of recent days. I stood on the threshold of another long canoe trip, but this time there was no guidebook to carry me safely from start to finish. I would rely instead on a combination of sources, not always complete or, as I would soon discover, accurate.

The put-in, where I would launch my canoe, lay an hour's drive away on dusty logging roads. My parents would drive me there later that morning, then meet me again in twelve days for a resupply.

The first twenty miles would take me through new territory—a straightforward twelve miles down the length of Seboomook Lake, followed by eight river miles with all those ledge drops near the start. That section of the West Branch, technically an alternate route of the NFCT, had always seemed steeped in mystery. Marked on the map with multiple symbols indicating rapids, it was seldom traversed by thru-paddlers. I had always been reluctant to attempt it, until I dreamed up this trip.

I dug through my stack to find NFCT Map 11 and unfolded it. This was one of a series of thirteen waterproof maps that cover the length of the trail. In addition to navigational help, the maps provide a wealth of information about the geology, history, and ecology of the waterway. My route this summer would cross parts of NFCT Maps 11 and 12 before entering what would be, for me, more uncharted territory.

From Seboomook Dam, the map explained, "a 0.75-mile section of flat water leads to the first of seven Class II–III ledge drop rapids, all of which should be scouted before running. All have easy portages around them and a gravel road along river right leads to the end of the rapids at the Roll Dam campsite."

The road, I thought, *I should try to find a better description of the road.*

A quick search on my laptop had led me to the American Whitewater website and the image at which I was now staring. Scrolling through the pages, my trepidation grew. Here, on a bright-green map, were twelve rapids, rather than the seven I'd expected. Phrases like "big, grabby hole" jumped out at me, and I wished fervently for a printer. *How had I missed researching this?* I copied the map as accurately as I could on a piece of paper.

"A great place for almost any boating skill level at the low summertime release level," said American Whitewater, which sounded more reassuring. "The drop and pool nature of this river is unlike most other New England rivers, which have long boulder-strewn rapids. Novice paddlers will find they can carry any or all the drops without bushwhacking several hundred yards. If they choose to run, the drops are intense but very short with a large slow recovery pool below."

I knew water levels in the river were at summertime lows. It was mid-July, and the season so far had been a dry one. The *AMC River Guide: Maine*, another resource that I would rely on, rates this stretch as Class III at low water, defined as a flow of 300 cubic feet per second (cfs) from the dam. American Whitewater did not recommend running this section below that flow.

I clicked the link to the dam's flow gauge to recheck current conditions. That morning, the dam was releasing only 198 cubic feet per second, a very low number, perhaps not even runnable. I would not have too much water, but would I have enough?

It was a sobering moment that made me question how prepared I was for this whole adventure. Taking a deep breath, I tried to put everything into perspective.

The lodge where we were staying was called The Birches. Since the 1930s, guests had been coming here in search of adventure and the peaceful renewal of nature. For my parents and me, this place was an old friend. We'd discovered it during Paddle for Hope, my 2011 kayaking fundraiser, and had returned often with family and friends. Here I'd taken the only rest day on my long thru-paddle.

Just across a narrow strip of grass, hidden now by the fog, lay the largest lake in Maine. When the sun broke through, there would be the distinctive profile of Mt. Kineo, with its sharp cliff and sloping shoulders, and the broad reach of Moosehead Lake. Here, naturalist and writer Henry David Thoreau and many others had begun their wilderness explorations. In their hearts, I'm sure, were many of the same feelings of doubt and uncertainty that I was trying hard to overcome.

On a map of Maine, Moosehead Lake is by far the largest body of freshwater. If you plunked it down in the center of the state, then gave it a good nudge toward the western border with Canada, you'd have it about right. The Northern Forest Canoe Trail follows the Moose River into Moosehead about midway up its western shore, then turns north up the lake for fifteen miles to Seboomook Point. There, the lake divides into two broad arms and the NFCT paddler can follow either.

The left arm leads to Northwest Carry and the right to Northeast Carry. Both are ancient portages that cross a slight height of land between watersheds, from the Kennebec into the Penobscot. Both bring paddlers to the West Branch of the Penobscot River.

The Penobscot watershed, Maine's largest, drains one-fourth of the state, an area of over 8,500 square miles. Rainwater and snowmelt from as far away as the Quebec border find their way to the distant Atlantic Ocean, in Penobscot Bay. From the north and west, the North and South Branches of the Penobscot flow into Seboomook

Lake. Below the dam at the east end of the lake, the West Branch emerges, to travel 117 miles to its meeting with the East Branch in Medway.

These are the ancestral lands of the Penobscot Indian Nation, whose reservation is on Indian Island, below the confluence of the East and West Branches. According to the Penobscot Nation, 1,224 lakes and 188 named rivers and streams, totaling 7,127 miles, are encompassed within this basin. The names of many, like Caucomgomoc, Kenduskeag and Nesowadnehunk, bear witness to the people who knew them first. For the next seventeen days, I would paddle and portage for 185 miles, crossing twenty-two rivers, streams, lakes, and ponds, and never leave this vast watershed.

A few hours later, my parents and I arrived at the "Twenty-Mile Checkpoint," one of the gates operated by a nonprofit corporation called North Maine Woods Inc. NMW manages access to over 3.5 million acres of land in northern Maine. This partnership among forest landowners of all sizes and Maine's natural resource agencies has simplified recreational use of these lands.

Most people enter NMW lands through gated checkpoints on the perimeter, like this one. This has eliminated the need for many interior gates. There are now uniform regulations and user fees across the properties of many different landowners. Ian, at work inside the rustic office, registered me for nine nights of camping along the Penobscot River Corridor and Allagash Wilderness Waterway, for a total cost of $68. On the Penobscot and Allagash, the state of Maine owns the river corridors and manages and patrols the waterways, while NMW collects the camping fees.

"I'm from Scotland, you know," Ian added with a smile, his accent truly leaving no doubt.

Pittston Farm, where I would put in at the western end of Seboomook Lake, dates to 1907. It was once a working farm, feeding the lumbermen and caring for the livestock of the Great Northern Paper Company. Now the site has a museum, historic buildings, campsites, and a restaurant.

By eleven o'clock, we were down at the boat launch. After freeing the boat from its straps, I took it to the lake, settling it gently at the water's edge. Empty, it weighed just thirty-two pounds. I went back and forth with gear, then carefully began to load the boat. It was the same lightweight canoe that had brought me safely through my NFCT thru-paddle, and everything had its place. I put the large green waterproof backpack with my tent and sleeping gear in the stern and the medium-sized blue and yellow dry bags with food, cooking gear, and clothing in the bow. A small orange dry bag held items like snacks, first aid kit, and camera that would need to be handy during the day. Dad watched silently until I finished, then walked with me back up to the truck, where I gave Mom a big hug. The time had come to say good-bye.

The first paddle strokes felt awkward and yet momentous. I was relieved to finally be starting, but my mind whirled, mentally checking that nothing had been forgotten. Where the road still hugged the lake, I could see that Mom and Dad had paused to watch me pass. I waved, but there was no way to know if they had seen. *I glided out into a still and quiet dream, back at last,* I wrote.

The sky, streaked with delicate, wispy cirrus clouds, hinted at rain ahead. Tomorrow, thunderstorms were forecast for much of the day. By noon, I had gone more than four miles, along a wild, sandy shoreline indented with many small coves and inlets. *Hello, Great Northern Diver.* The first loon of the trip hung close for a time, calling once from straight behind me. A family of mergansers erupted in flight, their white wing bars flashing.

My shoulders loosened, falling into a long familiar rhythm. Once more, the paddle took on a cadence of its own. With each stroke, the blade sent back a tiny whirlpool that danced and drifted, then faded quietly away. My thoughts wandered, and still I paddled on, keeping to my course.

Gradually a line of low hills rose to the south, and then the lake began to narrow. I searched the distant shore ahead for clues on where to go. From afar, layers of different colors and textures overlapped. A long finger of shaggy moss-green, topped with pointed fir, met the brilliant green of verdant marsh. Although there was nothing to indicate an opening, a continuation of the lake, I knew there must be one, and where the layers met, I would find it. Then, suddenly, the way resolved itself, like words jumping into meaning on a page.

I found a pebbled beach with sun for swimming and shade for lunch. The chicken legs, bread and butter, and oranges I ate were the last remnants of yesterday's picnic. Ten miles from the boat launch, I paddled onto NFCT Map 11, a milestone of sorts. By now, my ribs were aching. More than a month before, I'd bruised them in a fall. I could only hope the pain, just a nudge now, would not grow worse.

The solid bulwark of Seboomook Dam marked the unmistakable end of the lake. I glided to a stop at the concrete ramp of a boat launch on the left, just above a barrier of buoys. Climbing out, stretching stiff muscles, I reached to unclip one of the dry bags. This was it, the first step in the first of twenty-four, or likely far more, portages or carries that I anticipated making on this trip. Some would be clearly marked on the map. Others would arise from necessity.

Portages connect watersheds, bypass dams or rapids, and parallel rivers or streams when water levels are too high or low. In addition, upstream travelers must portage in other spots, where paddling would be delightful, if only they could go the other way.

Every portage brings plenty of opportunity for walking. Most of mine would be accomplished in two trips—one to carry the boat and one to ferry the rest of the gear. Long ago, someone came up with the brilliant idea of using a portage yoke—a piece of wood stretched across the width of the boat, often with a foam pad to cushion the shoulders—to make carrying more comfortable. Thanks to my dad, I had a custom portage yoke that he had built in his workshop, which had served me well on past trips.

After emptying the boat, I re-buckled my padded canoe chair upside down under the seat and out of the way. Then the yoke slipped neatly into the frame of the seat. Four small bungee cords secured both the yoke and my two double-bladed paddles in place, making the total load weight around 38 pounds. I wore my head net, as well as my PFD (personal flotation device or life jacket). I'd learned by experience that the portaging canoeist has no free hands to swat black flies or mosquitoes.

In *Upwards*, I recount the experience and emotion of my first traditional Adirondack carry:

Taking a deep breath, I reached for the gunwales and rolled the canoe up, with a little bounce. Another wiggle or two got it perfectly balanced, and I was off. This choreography would get smoother as the weeks went by, but even this first time, it worked.

There was something about my firm grasp on the thwart and the yoke settling solid on my shoulders that carried me back in time. As it has through the centuries, the trail ahead disappeared beneath the bow, shyly emerging a bit more with each careful step. The balance, the rhythm of the carry—look up to find the way, look down for sure footing—was repeated again and again, in a dance that connected me to all those who had ever gone this way before.

Most times, I took the load of gear first, allowing me to scout the portage route without a canoe on my head. I would then return empty-handed for the boat. On this first straightforward portage around Seboomook Dam, I shouldered the heavy backpack, got a firm grip on the rest of the dry bags, and headed up the gravel road. Just above the boat ramp, I discovered a beautifully clean lean-to, empty and inviting. Shaking off the temptation to stop for the day, I reminded myself of what lay ahead. The next few miles were going to take a while, whether I went by river or road, and the more I could get done today, the better.

By five o'clock, I had finished the short portage and committed myself to the river.

For safety, I was carrying a SPOT Gen 3 satellite messenger, with a 911 button for emergencies. That button, which I'd never had to use, would automatically summon all available rescue personnel, giving the exact coordinates of my position. The SPOT also had a tracking function, which would allow a small group of family and friends to closely follow my progress. Each night, I would send a message telling everyone that I was safely in camp. I had already told Dad that I would probably start down the river tonight and might end up stealth camping along the way.

"As long as you send an OK message tonight," he'd reassured me, "I'm not going to worry about you, even if you don't make it to an established campsite."

The river would descend forty-nine feet over the next two miles, dropping ten feet in the first mile and thirty-nine in the second.

Past these ledge drops I faced a big decision—
remain on the river or follow the road?

Everyone agreed that this section started quietly, with nearly a mile of flatwater. Wildlife was everywhere, and I enjoyed the brief, but peaceful, interlude. Kingfishers swooped and rattled along the shore and, again and again, flurries of splashing ducks took flight downriver.

At the first hint of whitewater, I hesitated a long time scouting what turned out to be just a small drop, easily runnable. When I arrived at the first set of real ledges, there was no doubt where I was. The AMC river guide warns paddlers that this spot, which they call Double Hydraulic, "sets the mood for the more difficult section below." I would agree.

A ledge stretched across the full width of the river, the dark smooth water above dropping ominously over the edge into a confusion of white. It was particularly turbulent and nasty looking in the center, where jagged rocks strained currents pouring over from two directions. There was another smaller ledge below. The right bank looked as though a giant had dropped an armload of massive building

at had landed helter-skelter along the shore. I scrambled up
blo r, lugging my gear, then the canoe. Simply getting to the por-
an rail was an accomplishment.

Back on the quiet water below the ledges, I drifted, putting off
e moment of decision. This was it. If I were going to escape the river,
the nearby trail would provide the only access to the road before the
river turned away. Downstream, what I could see looked enticingly
serene, and I knew that the next half-mile would be flatwater.

I deliberated, keenly aware that afternoon was slipping into evening. On the pro side, of course, I would be walking on a road, most
likely a quiet one. On the con side, darkness would no doubt fall before I could finish, forcing me to camp somewhere along the way. The
two-mile carry, I reminded myself, would mean six miles of walking,
as the boat made one load, the gear another, and I would need to walk
back empty-handed in between. Most importantly, if I went the easy
way, the mysteries ahead would remain mysteries, and I would only
know the ins and outs of some dusty gravel road. Plus, the portages
ahead were simple, everyone agreed.

With only a few second thoughts, I paddled past the trail that
marked the prudent, careful choice and pointed my bow downriver.

After a half-mile, the serious stuff began. I portaged several more
drops, the first on river left, the rest on river right. Scouting along one
or both shores would usually reveal a blue-blazed trail, well-marked
once you found it. After unloading the canoe, reaching the trail involved some acrobatic maneuvering and risky lifting and pulling. The
wet and slippery ledges often ended abruptly, plunging steeply to the
ground before reaching the trail. Once, I fell, turning my ankle with a
sharp twinge that left me gasping in surrender for a while, not moving until the pain subsided.

Thankfully, the trails themselves were mostly clear and soft underfoot. Where downed trees blocked the path, I lifted over. Where
the path dropped into a rocky ravine and up again, I followed. Always,
I found my way back to the river. The sun sank slowly to the horizon,
then slipped away.

On the threshold of darkness, the river softened. The sweep of branch and limb melted into the vastness of the ebony forest, but the waters would not slumber. Swirls of current, the music of falling water, the allure of rounding one more bend pulled me onward. I breathed in deeply. The pungent scents of fir and moldering leaves infused the air—wild and ancient, driving away the cobwebs of civilization.

There is a spirit that falls upon the rivers of the north in this last evening hour. The curtain of night is approaching, absolute and unstoppable. As the light fades, we journey on toward camp, hushed and awed by a place that stands as it has always done. Senses awaken and nerves tingle. This is not a feeling of not belonging, but rather an awareness of our tiny part in time and space.

I turned to look back to the west, from where I'd come. As if in blessing, the sun parted a halo of cloud to trace a shining path down the center of the river. At last, where the trail hugged a bluff above the next pair of spectacular ledge drops, the biggest yet, I stopped. A carpet of soft, dry pine needles and moss widened into a spot just big enough for my tent, and I would have the lullaby of rapids to sing me to sleep. It was a good place, one that I might have picked even if I weren't running out of daylight.

I sent a SPOT message to say that I was safely in camp. Then, staggering with weariness, I triaged the steps of setting up camp. Boat flipped high and dry near the end of the portage, with gear underneath. A quick swim and a change into clean camp clothes—long pants and a long-sleeved shirt to keep the bugs at bay. Tent up and the bear rope hung on the most dubious of trees, across an obviously dead branch that was the best I could find. Water filtered. Eating came last, and by then it was dark. Dinner after a long first day out was cheese, an apple, pepper slices, and cookies.

When I went to hang my food in total blackness, the limb broke, no surprise as it was both skinny and rotten. Probing farther afield with my flashlight, I settled for perching the bag in a thick-limbed spruce near the river's edge, at the perfect height for a bear buffet.

It wouldn't be the only chance I'd taken that day.

CHAPTER 2

CAPSIZED

Everyday courage has few witnesses. But yours is no less noble because no drum beats for you and no crowds shout your name.

—Robert Louis Stevenson

No one has ever died from a wild black bear attack in the state of Maine, according to the records of the Maine Department of Inland Fisheries and Wildlife.

Once, long ago, a baby did die in a fall from a horse-drawn carriage, after a bear spooked the horse. "That wouldn't qualify as a bear attack in my book," wrote MDIFW wildlife biologist and bear specialist Randy Cross, as he recounted the tragic story. I agree.

For years, I had been hoping to meet one of Maine's black bears, along a wild river shore or deep in the forest, preferably under circumstances where both of us felt safe. So far, the only one I'd seen in Maine had been a streak of black that shot across the arrow-straight Telos (*Tea*-loss) Road far ahead of our truck.

Most bears do their best to avoid encounters with humans. Although the state's black bear population has been steadily increasing, up from 23,000 in 2004 to 36,000 in 2015, Maine has a relatively low number of bear complaints, compared to other northeastern states. MDIFW attributes this, in part, "to bears being more common where human densities are lowest." In addition, Cross believes that intense hunting pressure over centuries has "weeded out more aggressive bears." This could help to explain why most people who venture into the wilds of Maine never see one.

Black bears should still be treated with great respect. According to MDIFW records and several additional incidents reported in the *Bangor Daily News*, there have been thirteen people injured in twelve bear attacks since 1984. Half of these incidents involved bears wounded or treed by hunters or attracted to bear baiting sites. Half of the rest involved food in some way. A young camper sleeping in the pants he'd worn to clean fish was bitten in the knee. A fisherman was aggressively pursued by a bear who had first eaten the bologna sandwich lunch he'd left on a stump. A teenager was knocked down while photographing a mother sow and cubs near his backyard bird feeder.

However, it was a June 1987 incident that I found the most alarming.

"A camper from Massachusetts was bitten on both knees by a bear that then tried to drag him out of his tent and into the woods near Baxter State Park," wrote John Holyoke, in a 2011 *Bangor Daily News* article. "The camper managed to scramble out of his sleeping bag as the bear dragged it—and him—toward the woods during the early-morning attack. The camper was treated at a hospital for puncture wounds to his legs, then returned to his campsite, retrieved his tent, and set it up again."

I sincerely hope that the bear had been relocated by that time!

I don't dwell on the thought of bears in camp, but, in the morning, I was relieved to see my food bag still perched on its vulnerable branch, undisturbed. Bears—and raccoons, skunks, mice, and squirrels—can be a problem, and part of my nightly backcountry camping routine is to hang any bags containing food and cooking gear well out of range. I usually locate a suitable tree branch and get the tricky rope deployment done early in the evening, in case it grows dark by the time I'm finished eating.

My tiny tent, a one-person Sierra Designs Flashlight 1 UL model, weighing just under three pounds, looked right at home tucked into the edge of the path, and I'd slept.

In the daylight, the rapids I was perched above looked even more awe inspiring. I guessed that one was the infamous E-Ledge, rated Class III+. From above, the river came curving unconcerned around an ordinary bend where deep forest blanketed the rocky shore. There, a mishmash of high ledges zigzagged across the river, stretching from bank to bank. A confusion of water boiled over into froth below. Midriver stood four large boulders, like teeth in the jaws of destruction.

By seven o'clock, my canoe lay waiting patiently at the end of the portage with its load thoroughly secured. The rocks here were sculpted into fanciful shapes and decorated with lichens, colored dark somber green and vibrant orange. Their appearance suited the mood of this wild place.

Mornings are my time of strength and rosy optimism. I felt energized, ready to confront the challenges that remained between me and safety. I could easily have let fear prevail. These drops were far beyond the abilities of me in my boat, especially at the current low water level. Everything had to be carefully scouted. Not just the most difficult drops, but anything hidden around a bend in the river.

On the lower ledges, probably letters G through K, I found no portage trails. None at all. For three hours, I lugged my boat and gear over ledges and wiggled my way through thick stands of young conifers. Somewhere along the way, it began to rain.

At one of the first rapids, I decided that river left looked better, but *better* was a relative term. I maneuvered my boat along the shore for a while, tossing my bags gently from ledge to ledge, then pulling, lifting, and wiggling the boat along to the next pocket of water. Finally, I came to a tall rock that would have taken me straight up.

To get around this spot, I would have to go through the woods. I had two choices to get there. Either scramble across a mat of tangled logs reminiscent of a beaver lodge or climb down and then up a steep slope. Lugging enough gear that my balance was iffy, I struggled up the slope, through the thick young forest, over a giant downed tree, and with relief plunked my bags down on gravel below the drop. Then I made another trip. Walking back, my river shoes slid right out from under me, and I went down, no doubt adding to my colorful collection of bruises. My canoe was not going to make it up that slope.

The maze of logs was a flatter option, and I could drag the boat across. I stepped gingerly, aware of the hazard of falling through. I made it, without slipping again, then wove my boat through the puzzle of stems, backward and forward, twisting and turning to navigate through the closely packed trees. At last, gear, boat, and I were reunited, and another of the mysterious lettered ledges was behind me.

Just as life can be defined by moments of deep meaning, time on the river cannot be solely measured in miles or hours, but in the magnitude of delight or struggle. The effort that went into working my way around just one of the rapids was multiplied several times over.

Near the end, courage and frustration, and the intermittent rain, coaxed me into running first one, then a couple more, tricky spots. By now, I had no idea which letter, if any, might be attached to them, but it was a lot more fun to hurtle forward through the most likely slot and emerge unscathed a moment later. After scouting and mentally choosing my line, the river would grab me, my heart racing. Then came the plunge, the bow burying itself, then it was free, and I was turning and floating into the eddy.

At last, my GPS map showed the Roll Dam campsite just ahead, the finish line of surviving this dubious undertaking. The moment when I had decided not to take a flat, gravel road for two miles seemed eons ago, and I had had quite an education since then. Beyond one final drop, I could see a much gentler river curve away into the distance. There was the West Branch that I knew and loved.

The ledge below looked just like the two that I had just run, though perhaps a bit higher. I knew I could do it, and then I'd be finished at last!

I gave myself plenty of space, lined up on the right, and went for it. I was over the drop, when suddenly the boat pulled to the right and simply flipped. Still grasping the paddle, I was pulled under and the river closed above me. Churning water gripped me, resisting, clutching, holding me, and I felt a flash of fear. When I came up and tasted air, the canoe was on its side, then upright, cooperating of its own accord with our rescue. Perhaps a third full of water, it looked forlorn with the tent bag trailing behind. We swam together, a jumble of boat and bags, rope and paddle.

Keep your feet up, I thought, remembering the danger of getting a foot wedged between underwater rocks. Slowly, I kicked toward the bank. Later, I would discover that the river had stolen my head net, but not much else. Thankfully, the GPS and SPOT had been zipped into my PFD pockets, a precaution I would take through all significant whitewater. Hands shaking, shivering more from the scare than the cold water, I bailed out the canoe and clipped everything back in its place.

The Roll Dam campsite, broad and inviting, with mown grass and a lean-to, popped into sight around the very next curve. What a decision—stay here, regroup, and dry out or continue downstream? Wet and chilled, standing in the rain, I looked long and hard at the dry spacious lean-to. It was only late morning, though, and I returned to the river.

Something else was pushing me onward—a long-awaited visit and the possibility of a thick, juicy cheeseburger and warm drink, not too far ahead. Old friends Ed and Shirley Raymond had a country store along the historic Northeast Carry, near Moosehead Lake. Just five peaceful miles downriver, then a two-mile walk across the carry. I hadn't seen them now for three summers, and it was a given that I would try to stop in today. With luck, they would be there and not gone to a doctor's appointment, which happened more often these days.

A mature bald eagle, the first I'd seen with regal snow-white head and tail, brightened the dreary day, and the river miles passed uneventfully. Soon, I was pulling my boat up, out of sight from the river, gear stowed tidily underneath. Before I left, I dug out some dry clothes and crammed them into my smallest dry bag, to carry with me.

The rain persisted, but the walking warmed me, and it didn't seem too much of a chore. There was a harvesting operation in full swing along the carry, a nice thinning job, where some trees were removed and the nicest left to grow larger.

The store turned out to be open, hallelujah!

I pulled open the door with great relief and there was Ed, looking the same as ever, sitting intent over some reading at one of the tables. Otherwise, the store, with its well-stocked shelves, was empty.

He looked up and smiled, seemingly not alarmed that I was dripping on his floor. Behind his glasses, his kindly eyes looked pleased to see me. It had been a while, but I knew he recognized me.

"Hi, Ed! I'm on another long canoe trip and couldn't pass by without walking up to visit you and Shirley."

Since no one else was there, I asked if I could change. In the small front room, out of sight around the corner, I stripped off my sodden river clothes and wiggled into blessedly dry long underwear and warm wool socks.

Back behind the counter, Ed was already at the stove, making me a cheeseburger, and the tea water was heating. When Shirley came in, she had a smile to match Ed's, and kindly offered to dry my clothes. Next thing I knew, I was wearing a large purple sweatshirt with a moose on it, and all my wet stuff was in her dryer, even my raincoat and bathing suit.

My friends looked well and active, and Ed admitted that he was "in better spirits."

There were fewer visitors these days, though, in all the seasons. In fact, no one at all came into the store while I was there, and I hoped that the two of them were getting along all right.

"I thought when they opened that seven-forty," said Ed, referring to the Northern Forest Canoe Trail, "people would come." Like me, he was surprised that more folks weren't coming through.

One person he had recently seen was my friend Peter Macfarlane, who stopped in back in May.

Five years earlier, Peter had successfully thru-paddled the NFCT from west to east, the direction that most people do, finishing in twenty-eight days. Peter is a canoe builder, with a Vermont business called Otter Creek Smallcraft. He traveled in one of his own cedar strip canoes and took no wheels, carrying his boat and gear in a single trip across the many miles of portages.

Personally, I owed Peter a huge debt of gratitude. On my thru-paddle, he and Dan Brown, a 2014 thru-paddler, had accompanied me across the wide, windy open expanse of Lake Champlain. Peter had helped me with my paddling technique and continued with me up the first few miles of Vermont's Missisquoi River, showing me the nuances of making progress upstream.

If anyone could make it in the other direction, it would be Peter. On May 14, 2018, he left Fort Kent, Maine, in the same canoe, with the goal of going the other way in the same amount of time. Instead of 150 upstream miles, he would face more than 250. On the sixth day of his "backwards" thru-paddle, the sun had shone, but he'd battled strong headwinds to struggle up the West Branch to Northeast Carry. He, too, had devoured one of Shirley's delicious cheeseburgers before launching into crashing surf on Moosehead, continuing his quest to write his name into the annals of NFCT history.

In the winter, Ed and Shirley feed the deer, who come faithfully into their yard day after day. Last winter, the herd had included a three-legged doe that Ed had pampered a bit, making sure she always got her share of food. On the store counter was a jar to collect money for the deer food, and I gladly added my change.

As it turned out, if I'd stayed at the Roll Dam lean-to, I would have missed my visit. Ed and Shirley planned to be away the following day, attending to some business in town. We visited for quite a while, and I stayed even longer to write, while my camera battery charged. At last, I knew I should be going.

"You're an angel!" I told Shirley. Even my bathing suit was warm as I pulled it back on.

The sky had brightened, and a breeze sprang up to discourage the mosquitoes, as I retraced my steps. The last part of Northeast Carry follows a dirt track from the main gravel road to the river. In past years, it had been passable with a four-wheel drive truck. Now, deep ruts and giant puddles barred the way, and I wouldn't want to attempt it. It appeared that the road was no longer being maintained.

Along that rough section, not far from the river, I stopped to fill my water bottles at a spring that Ed said was "as sweet as any." Things were looking up.

Back on the river, I spotted an osprey in a dead tree. After another couple of quiet miles, I turned up Lobster Stream, where a beaver cut a long, thin V as he swam across in front of the canoe, then tail-slapped and dove. I fought a headwind out of the south all the way to the first campsite on Lobster Lake, to the right, at the end of aptly named Shallow Bay. This was simply a short side trip to camp for the night. In the morning, I would return to the West Branch.

The site was empty, high, and wooded, with beaches on two sides of the small point. Right away, I emptied all my bags and started laying things out to dry. From some, a small stream of water poured out. No sooner was everything spread out, then the rumble of distant thunder sent me scrambling to pack up. When the rain began, it never let up, continuing into the night. For a second evening, I had no campfire or hot food, though thankfully, I'd had my burger.

I slept more than ten hours, waking often to shift my aching body, then drifting back to oblivion. The morning was cloudy, damp, and dismal. *I know that drama makes a good story*, I thought, *but please no drama today.* The river route ahead was simple, returning up Lobster Stream and turning east down the West Branch, where I would have a broad selection of campsites, starting about ten miles along.

About halfway across Shallow Bay, I spotted a young moose. For a time, she simply tracked my progress. Then, nervously, she moved deeper into the shoreline bushes, her ears the last to disappear.

Coming up Lobster Stream, the weather was still gloomy, the clouds thick. An older man in a rough plaid shirt and suspenders slowed and waved as he passed me from behind in a metal skiff. The harsh smell of fuel lingered even after the sound of the motor had faded.

Soon he was back, though, a smiling woman with short gray hair and a bright-blue shirt perched in the bow, adding a bit of color to the day.

"Have fun!" I shouted.

"I plan to!" she answered cheerily.

By the time I left Lobster Stream, bits of blue sky were appearing to the north. *Enough to patch a Dutchman's britches*, my mother would have said. Soon, there was blessed sun.

This section of the West Branch has hundreds of submerged logs, left from the days of the huge river drives, and vast beds of underwater plants streaming with the current. It's always a good stretch for finding moose. After passing under the last bridge that I'd see for a while, I stopped on an island campsite. I boiled water for some beef noodle soup; today, I would be sure of at least a hot lunch.

By the time I heard approaching voices, my gear was spread far and wide to dry, taking up much of the space. I wondered if they'd been planning to stop for lunch, but the large group of boys, from Pine Island Camp on Belgrade Lakes, had just put in and were eager to keep on going.

All day I paddled into a headwind, out of the north now, the opposite of the previous evening.

"Some people let things just ruin their day," I remembered Ed saying yesterday. "Take this rain."

Well, the wind today was no different. I went with it or against it, I suppose, appreciated the sheltered spots, and reached for inner calm. I reminded myself that there wasn't far to travel to the cluster of campsites around Big Island. I focused on the movement of the stately spruce and fir against billowy clouds and deep blue sky, looking for the prettiest framing of trees against sky.

On a high grassy bank, a showy Canada lily caught my eye. From one tall stem hung five golden flowers, their heads bowed, and five unopened buds. Inside each large flower were splotches of darker orange, matched in color by the drooping stamens. Waving heads of feathery grass, a delicate pinkish green, and brighter pink swamp milkweed completed the little garden.

Then I looked downriver and, just like that, there was another moose, bathed in sun. Had she come out while I'd been admiring the flowers? Or had she been there all along?

As I drew closer, she began to walk toward me along the shore, warily watching me. Her ears did a dance, twitching and shaking in constant motion against the bugs. Nearer to me, she waded into the river, deeper and deeper, until I realized she was going to swim across behind me. On the other shore, she emerged, hair glistening dark with water, and walked calmly into the woods. Good-bye, Moose #2.

After Moosehorn Stream, the current quickened, and I hung up on an unseen rock. It was time to wake up! Out in the current, a small brown piece of wood floated, but not downstream. It was a red squirrel, calmly swimming a straight course toward the far shore. He

An attractive West Branch campsite adjacent to Ragmuff Stream

climbed out and shot into the woods. By late afternoon, I was settled at the Big Ragmuff campsite, beside lively Ragmuff Stream, which pleased me. I had camped there with my son Taylor long ago, on my first trip down the West Branch.

The last campers, however, did not please me. They had left behind tons of trash. In the fire pit, which was full to the brim, I found burned cans and even glass, twisted into crazy shapes by the heat. The grassy site was littered with caps, wrappers, green plastic dental flossers, and an assortment of odd pieces of rope and string. I also found a quarter, which I guess was my tip for cleaning up the mess.

It turned out to be a lovely evening. I toasted sandwich thins on the campfire and slathered them with the last of the butter and some honey. Along with cheese, carrots, tea, and mints, that was supper. Even though I could have, I didn't feel like cooking pasta or potatoes after all.

The moon, grown now to a perfect half circle, kept company with countless stars, while the fire of my own creation sank into a bed of glowing coals.

CHAPTER 3

THE WILD, RUGGED WAY

Since the glaciers retreated 12,000 years ago, these waterways and associated resources—the scenery, geology, flora and fauna, night skies, and more—have attracted people to this area. Native Americans still cherish these resources. Lumberjacks, river drivers, and timber owners have earned their livings here. Artists, authors, scientists, conservationists, recreationists, and others have drawn knowledge and inspiration from this landscape.

—**Barack Obama**, *Presidential Proclamation:*
Establishment of the Katahdin Woods and Waters National Monument

There was a purpose to this odyssey, I promise, beyond my need to immerse myself once more in the exhilarating drama of a long canoe expedition. The planning had begun at the end, with a compelling destination. From there, the route had almost crafted itself over the past months.

Winters in Maine can be treacherous that way. We spend long hours dreaming by the woodstove, the days cut short by darkness. Our treasured lakes transform into icy, windswept prairies over which we wistfully gaze. Canoes lie buried beneath mounds of snow, while we long for the simple joy of bare brown ground. All that time, plans for the short, glorious summer grow ever more ambitious.

For such a wild, undeveloped state, Maine has very little federal land. Nine out of every ten acres statewide are forested, the highest percentage in the nation. Surprisingly, though, the only national forest land is a relatively small part of the White Mountain National Forest in western Maine. Much of the void is filled by large expanses of state land, well managed, accessible, and priceless. The crown jewel of these is Baxter State Park, home to the state's highest peak, Katahdin.

What Maine's federal holdings lack in quantity, though, they make up for in quality. The state's only national park, Acadia, is a place of breathtaking beauty where the sun first touches America on the top of Cadillac Mountain, high above the rugged, rocky coast. Its one national scenic trail, the Appalachian Trail, and one national wild and scenic river, the Allagash Wilderness Waterway, have become icons of our country's outdoor sporting heritage. Then, not long ago, Maine got its first national monument. Not a stone memorial or statue, but a wild treasure almost twice as large as Acadia National Park.

Ever since, I'd wanted to explore it.

I would paddle to the national monument, I decided, along an imaginative route. It would be 150 miles by canoe just to reach the monument boundary. It felt right to come there partly by way of the Northern Forest Canoe Trail. Ultimately, I would experience anew many of the hallmarks of my thru-paddle: upstream travel through rapids, arduous carries, steep portage accesses, and battles with the foes of wind and weather on remote wilderness lakes. The landscapes, the wildlife, and the history would be there, too.

My journey would also touch upon the Allagash Wilderness Waterway, Baxter State Park, and the Thoreau–Wabanaki Trail, which follows the routes of Thoreau's 1846, 1853, and 1857 trips to the north Maine woods. In the first, he climbed Katahdin, and in the second and third, he canoed and portaged much of my intended route. Thoreau's book, *The Maine Woods*, encompasses all three of those journeys.

The Thoreau–Wabanaki Trail, an initiative of the nonprofit organization Maine Woods Forever, promotes not only the history, but the spiritual and cultural aspects of Thoreau's journeys, particularly through his interactions with his two Penobscot Indian guides. Maine Woods Forever has published two trail maps, one an overview of the entire trail and one for the East Branch of the Penobscot River, which I would utilize later in my travels.

Another excellent book, *The Wildest Country: Exploring Thoreau's Maine*, by J. Parker Huber, provides a wealth of detail from the author's travels along these routes, as well as Thoreau's original accounts. In my writing, I will touch upon Thoreau when the moment inspires comment but will not attempt to recreate what has already been done so well.

On August 24, 2016, in conjunction with the commemoration of the National Park Service's 100th anniversary, President Barack Obama designated 87,563 acres east of Baxter State Park as Katahdin Woods and Waters National Monument. He was able to do this, unilaterally, because of a 110-year-old piece of legislation called the Antiquities Act of 1906.

In the early twentieth century, President Theodore Roosevelt and others were concerned about the disturbance and looting of southwestern archaeological sites. Working with Congress, Roosevelt developed a more streamlined avenue for preserving areas of historic or archaeological significance. They called the law the Antiquities Act and the preserves that it created national monuments.

National monuments differ from national parks in the method of their creation, rather than their management. National parks come into being when Congress passes a bill, and the president signs it into law. National monuments are created solely by presidential proclamation.

Since Teddy Roosevelt, every president except Richard Nixon, Ronald Reagan, and George H.W. Bush has taken advantage of the Antiquities Act to preserve additional federal lands. Barack Obama alone initiated or expanded a whopping thirty-four national monuments during his years in the White House.

On October 26, 2018, President Donald Trump designated his first national monument, honoring black Union soldiers of the Civil War, and their training grounds at Kentucky's 380-acre Camp Nelson. Ironically, national monuments had come under intense scrutiny not long before, when President Trump issued Executive Order 13792 on April 26, 2017. The order charged Interior Secretary Ryan Zinke with reviewing twenty-seven monuments, considering such diverse criteria as appropriate historical classification; impacts on multiple use; concerns of state, tribal, and local governments; and the availability of federal resources to manage the lands.

The list of monuments under review was released on May 5, 2017. Included was the newly created Katahdin Woods and Waters National Monument, in a separate table with the heading: "National monuments being reviewed to determine whether the designation or expansion was made without adequate public outreach and coordination with relevant stakeholders." Zinke visited Katahdin Woods and Waters on June 14 and issued his recommendations on August 24. For Maine's national monument, the news was good. The monument would not be impacted.

And so, this journey was born, its purpose to explore these new lands gifted to the people of Maine and our nation. To get there, I had chosen a route that few others would probably ever follow, certainly not the most direct way to reach the monument.

At Big Ragmuff, I woke to one of the heaviest dews I could ever remember. The tent was soaked and dripping. I moved it and my sleeping pad into the sun to dry while I visited the outhouse, which had a great ambiance. The lyrical notes of a hermit thrush, ferns in profusion, and sun filtering down to brighten the forest floor made a good start to the morning.

I thought about the day ahead, which would end in new waters. I would follow the familiar West Branch into the northwestern corner of Chesuncook Lake, then turn north up Caucomgomoc (*Cawk-ma-go-mick*) Stream for the first time.

Years before, the owner of The Birches, John Willard, had taken Dad and me up in his floatplane for a look at some of the places we'd canoed and camped over the years. We'd taken off from Moosehead, roared over Lobster Lake and down the West Branch to Chesuncook, where we'd turned up Caucomgomoc Stream into Black Pond, searching for moose in the shallows below. In the lime green of the marshes, a network of animal trails crisscrossed the wetlands, and we had seen several moose.

Not far downstream from Big Ragmuff, I discovered the group from Pine Island packing up, at a roomy, attractive campsite on Big

Exploring Thoreau's Pine Stream

Island. With the helpful current, I had gone six miles in two hours by the time that they caught up to me. You sure could hear those five canoes full of boys coming from a long distance away. We talked back and forth as we paddled, discovering that we would be taking the same route into the Allagash. The campers were from all over the states and even London.

Nearing Chesuncook Lake, I turned right to explore a tributary named Pine Stream. In September 1853, Thoreau's companion, George Thatcher, had killed a moose along its banks, and the group had camped there overnight. I found the first glance rather unappealing. Shaggy spruce overhung marled clay banks coated a slimy green. Tracks were everywhere, though, and it looked like a good spot for moose.

I went about a mile, until I found my way blocked by a rock ledge with water cascading over in a tiny waterfall. It was time to turn around. On the way in, I'd come upon a group of seven fluffy baby ducks, their heads striped yellow and brown, with no mother in sight. I'd suspected a tragedy, so it was a relief coming out to see a black duck mother leading the chevron of little ones firmly to safety. Quickly I counted them—yes, there were still seven.

Hungry, I pulled into the next campsite for lunch. There, I discovered a familiar mess. The fire pit was full of burned cans and the grass scattered with trash, including the identical green plastic dental flossers as at Big Ragmuff. It was the same rude people. I picked up everything, adding it to my bulging trash bag, although this time there was no tip.

There was no way I wanted to carry extra trash for the next fifty miles. I would need to stop at Chesuncook Village, about a mile off my planned route, to try to get rid of it.

Was I crazy to have collected trash that the rangers would probably have picked up anyway?

As I paddled toward the Chesuncook Village beach, I answered my own question. *What if this was a family's first wilderness canoe trip and they saw that mess?* I couldn't have just left it.

At the beach, I was relieved to meet two young people in a golf cart, who willingly took the heavy bag. I thanked them, then turned into the wind, headed for new territory. I would be going north into the upper reaches of the Penobscot watershed, while the route of the West Branch goes south, through Chesuncook into Ripogenus Lake. From there, the West Branch flows southeast, providing some of the best Class V whitewater rafting in the state before joining the East Branch in Medway.

I looked for Caucomgomoc Stream just north of the mouth of the West Branch. Where green bushes on a muddy bank overlapped a light sandy beach, I found the entrance to the stream. This is the start of an age-old route into the Allagash through Allagash Lake. Described on NFCT Map 12, this quiet, remote loop provides an alternative to the arduous Mud Pond Carry that I had followed twice before. Both lead to Chamberlain Lake. From there, I would cross the northern end of Baxter State Park, through Grand Lake Matagamon, to the East Branch. The national monument was still ninety miles ahead.

Quickly, I turned the corner into the stream.

Wham! A much stronger headwind, funneled down the wide channel, stopped me abruptly in my tracks. For the moment, I gave in and angled backward to a small beach to rest for a minute.

Perusing the map, I decided to follow the left shore, which appeared to be the most direct and sheltered choice. Instead, I kept finding myself drawn into dead-end side channels, perhaps because lake water levels were lower than normal. My ribs ached, and I felt intimidated by the stream's confusing patterns, when on the map it all looked simple.

Any campsite would look good right now, I thought, as I kept going, gradually moving upstream. The map showed just one site, about two miles above the lake. I prayed it would be empty.

It was. When I reached the spot, there were two sites on a gorgeous point. Both were empty. Both were clean. Even better, the skies were clear, and it was a reasonable four thirty in the afternoon.

A moose has come out, feeding off a point across from camp. All chores must stop. The water there is shallow, and she wanders around, tasting here and there. In a bath of late sun, her face is a noticeably lighter brown than her body. She is far, just a small dark moose shape in a vast landscape of river and marsh, edged by woods. Later she walks the shore, coming closer. Then I look once more, and she is swimming to my side. Her ears twitch in constant motion. I watch her for hours until she circles back to where she started.

In the margin of my journal, I noted Moose #3.

A cormorant sunned his wings on a river rock. Here in Maine, folks call these birds *shags.* An elusive quick-diving duck was hardly above the water, then gone so fast that I doubted for a moment that I'd really seen him. There were beaver, too, across from the second campsite. The pair were unaware of a watcher and nuzzled each other, relaxed and at peace. A host of red squirrels scampered about, scolding, and a kingfisher left no doubt that the horizontal branch at the edge of camp was his.

Tonight, I could feel myself settling into the journey. I had the energy to cook chicken and pasta, with oranges. My gear was tidy and dry, firewood stacked, water purified. It helped that it wasn't raining.

I thought again about all that trash, unable to get the picture out of my mind. It was sad that people with that lack of respect would come here. Even deeper than respect, what this place demanded was reverence—a true appreciation for its intrinsic value, generously shared. To have earned this place through hard work, courage, and endurance was truly a gift.

In the newness of morning, I awoke feeling just as appreciative. It was sunny and dry, and the wind was from the south. I would have a tailwind for a change. There had been an owl in the night, not long after midnight. It hooted one, two, three…four…five, over and over. A great horned owl, I thought.

On the map, this site was called Canvas Dam. Just beyond camp, I passed the remains of the old dam. A row of timbers tilted in formation, facing a pile of rock on the opposite shore. Almost immediately, I saw one of last night's beaver, then an osprey diving after fish. Ahead, a loon called, heralding the lake to come. Black Pond, a couple of miles upstream, would provide a five-mile respite before I faced the next upstream challenge.

On the right, a dark rock in a sea of grass had the vague shape of a moose's back. As I drew closer, I found Moose #4 feeding in the shallows behind the grassy point. When she noticed me, she strode firmly away to safety. In the distance, where the stream flowed from the lake, a mountain stood framed between two points, and I wondered if I was seeing faraway Allagash Mountain.

The shallow waters of Black Pond teemed with waterfowl—black ducks and a family of ring-necked ducks, the babies still fluffy. The lake's low water exposed wide swaths of beach and marsh. On the west shore, a blob of light tan looked different from the dark color of a moose. It was a whitetail doe, well out into the water. She was feeding, not drinking. Like a moose, she rooted around, browsing the underwater plants, then emerging with green strands dripping down. This was the first time I'd seen this, and I watched her for a long time. The sounds of her movement carried clearly over the water.

After quite a while, she became aware of my presence. She leaped and snorted, ran, then stopped in her tracks to look back. Again, she snorted twice, whirled in the other direction, stopped, snorted, then finally disappeared. She was not happy that I'd disturbed her.

There were two more moose, the last one unconcerned and reluctant to abandon the prime feeding spot that blocked the way I had to go. I lingered for a while, then snuck quietly by.

It was noon, and Black Pond was rapidly narrowing. Somewhere ahead, I would return to ascending Caucomgomoc Stream. The water grew deeper, and I filtered drinking water from the boat, amazed at how much easier it was than crouched over on the shore. The day was already mercilessly hot, and I knew that I needed to stay hydrated.

At first it was an easy paddle, with an attractive shoreline and a growing number of rocks. On one stood a yellowlegs, a bird that I'd only seen once before in these northern waters. My destination for the night, the dam on Caucomgomoc Lake, was about two miles away when the tempo of the stream began to change. This was not a surprise. I was approaching the one-and-a-half-mile portage to the dam, which followed a woods trail and then a logging road. The portage began at a campsite somewhere ahead on the left.

Some sources indicated that it was better to bypass the campsite, however, and keep to the stream for as long as possible before leaving it. The AMC river guide notes, "The rapids in Caucomgomoc Stream are easy enough that you can pull up the stream if you have enough water. The only difficulty—going up- or down-stream, is a ledge approximately two-thirds up the stream, about opposite where the trail joins the logging road. When you first see the ledge, take out on the left up a steep bank to the trail leading to the logging road." Later, I was to learn from other longtime guides that the section ahead, which they called "The Horserace," was better avoided.

After lunch, I tracked upstream through rapids for a tenth of a mile or so, to deeper, quieter waters. I was so proud of myself, having no idea what was coming. The stream curved away enticingly between high grassy banks. If I faced a problem ahead, I imagined running out of water, and I honestly didn't look very hard for the portage trail.

What I soon found were more lively rapids.

I hadn't seen the campsite and wondered if walking up rapids with everything in my boat, in one trip, wouldn't be simpler anyway on this sweltering afternoon. The rushing water felt cool and refreshing, much more pleasant than some hot buggy trail. I went on. Flowery midstream islands made good spots to take a break and walk for a while out of the strong current.

On the gravel bar below one island, a sudden commotion pulled my thoughts back to the present. My heart jumped. There was loud splashing and a brown shiny something scrambling and tumbling right at my feet. A spray of water droplets exploded in a frenzy. It was a beaver, struggling to get leverage, rolling and twisting, then becoming liquid grace the moment he reached the water.

Now I wouldn't have seen that on a logging road.

The river curved, a lot, and it felt like I walked two miles or more, mostly through Class I rapids. After a while, the current midstream became too strong to cross, and I was stuck on the right shore, away from the logging road. Once, I tried crossing at an island, but the water beyond it was deep. Delicately, I took just one more step, willing my foot to stay safe on the streambed. The current pulled me with incredible force. I hung, indecisive and terrified, in the center, then retreated as carefully as I'd advanced. The right bank it would be, for now anyway.

I fell many times and was surprised at how the rules from my thru-paddle quickly returned. Try to always hold onto something along the bank, a live branch or something rock solid. Choose each step with care. When you can, sit on a rock to rest a moment and then pull the boat by. Concentrate on where you are now—this step, working your way around this strainer—not on what lies ahead.

This part of Caucomgomoc Stream was as difficult as anything on the Northern Forest Canoe Trail. I knew I'd been careless to get caught up in exploring, getting a good story, fighting upstream, being a contrarian as usual. I took no photos, did no journaling, and don't know how many bends I rounded, hoping for calmer water. My body was battered, my energy drained, when I came at last to a high ledge. I would call it a waterfall. Even I have limits, and I had reached them.

CHAPTER 4

JEWEL OF THE ALLAGASH

To know what you prefer instead of humbly saying Amen to what the world tells you that you ought to prefer, is to have kept your soul alive.

—Robert Louis Stevenson, *An Inland Voyage*

There was no way I was going to pull up and over that ledge. To reach the portage, I would have to cross to the opposite bank. Luckily, the stream seemed slower and deeper here below the small falls. I went slowly, wading at an angle toward a small opening where I could pull my boat up on shore. Above, the bank rose steeply for quite a distance.

I perched dry bags and gear among the shoreline rocks, where they wouldn't fall in, then started to scramble up, tugging the canoe behind. After making some progress, I tied the bow line to a tree while I rested. This was a trick I'd learned on the NFCT. The goal was to avoid sliding back down and having to start over. Fighting to keep my feet on the slippery slope, I gradually hauled the heavy weight up, up, up, until at last the canoe rested on level ground.

Getting the gear up was simpler. When I was done and everything was piled safely around the canoe, a wave of relief washed over me. Shrugging the strain out of my shoulders, I looked straight down at the rushing water below, thankful indeed. I had survived my reckless decision to pull up Caucomgomoc Stream, and the portage trail must be close by.

Empty-handed, I wove through the thick young forest, thinking it might be a tight fit for my boat. Almost immediately, though, I came out on a well-worn trail paralleling the river. Turning right, I soon came to a short path connecting to the logging road. Not only was I safe, but I knew for sure where I was.

Imagine my amazement to soon hear voices from the direction of the stream. My first thought was fishermen, but it was the Pine Island boys, coming upriver in the same way that I had. I shouted down to let them know that the road was nearby. They hauled out, too, and together we trudged along, portaging a half-mile or more to several campsites just before the dam. NFCT Map 12 incorrectly shows the campsites on the far side of the dam.

Later, rereading the AMC river guide, I began to realize that my crazy stunt was what they recommended. I had indeed pulled up the stream to a ledge, then climbed a steep bank to find the trail to the logging road. In retrospect, I was glad I had gone that way.

I wouldn't have wanted to miss that beaver.

That evening, I barely had energy to pump water or cook dinner. To give the campers room, I squeezed into a small site by the stream, setting up my tent almost touching the picnic table. It didn't matter, though. I spent most of my time stretched out on my soft sleeping bag, unmoving.

My thoughts turned to the changes I could feel happening within myself. It was good to go to a place where I must rely solely on myself to get safely to camp. To rediscover and trust my own strength of will and body. To encounter new lands and waters, read their moods, and let experience and intuition guide me. I was surprised, too, how often I was reminded of places and challenges I'd seen before.

Ciss Stream was a prime example. By seven the next morning, I was crossing a small corner of Caucomgomoc Lake and turning up the wide, slow-moving stream. I paddled almost effortlessly, the current against me barely noticeable. This was the fen of Vermont's Clyde River, recreated.

I followed a winding, watery ribbon through a sea of green. Glossy red-winged blackbirds bent the stems of waving grass, then flashed away with their distinctive *chick-chick-chick* to another perch. Giant twisted stumps dotted the landscape, reaching skyward with weathered gray arms. Sometimes the horizon ahead seemed solid green, and I wondered where the stream could go. The backwards streaming of underwater plants gave one clue. Where the waving dance was strongest, so was the current. Ahead, a line of trees traced the edge of the marsh, another hint of the channel's path.

Moose #7 was in water up to her shoulders, and close before I noticed her. Again, I wanted to leave her feeding for the boys behind me to enjoy, but she had other plans. Quickly, she headed for shallower water and walked away, her feet making loud slurping, sucking sounds that carried over the quiet marsh. I willed her to come back every time she paused, but soon the forest had swallowed her up.

Five miles of meanders brought me to Round Pond, its waters a deep blue, ringed by dark-green forest rising into the hills. I turned my bow to the northeast. I knew just where I was headed.

I'd discovered Loon Lodge on the map, then come to know its inspiring history through outdoor writer George Smith's book, *Maine Sporting Camps*. Most Maine sporting camps have long, historic heritages, making Loon Lodge rather unique. In the mid-1980s, a couple, aged twenty-two and twenty, decided to move to Maine and fulfill their dream of buying and running a sporting camp.

When Mike and Linda Yencha found existing camps prohibitively expensive, they decided to build their own. Leasing land from a paper company, they set to work to construct their first cabin, then a second. Each year they added more buildings. Often, a cabin would have been booked at a spring outdoor show, and the race was on to have it completed in time.

Their first deer hunting season, some guests chose to purchase their meals, too, an option which is called the American plan. Preparing and serving meals would require a lodge as well as cabins.

"While I cut down spruce trees on the site and cleared the land," Mike remembers, "Linda went to work peeling logs, 120 of them! The poor girl had a pair of jeans and sweatshirt that could stand by themselves from all the sap on them when she was done with this daunting task. Plus let me point out that we had no running water for showers or baths." After their generator broke, "every board, log,

[and] sheet of plywood needed to be cut with the chainsaw." With the help of Linda's parents, the twenty-by-forty-foot lodge went up and was finished with a week to spare before the start of deer season.

Mike and Linda ran Loon Lodge for twenty-five years before moving to Alaska, where they purchased a fly-in-only fishing lodge. Loon Lodge was left in good hands with the new owners, Ray and Leslie Cooley, who still lease their land from Seven Islands Land Company. Nowadays, visitors can stay year-round in four of the original cabins and, from May until December, eat in that lodge, built of rough-sawn lumber and hand-peeled logs. For me, Loon Lodge had shone as a bright spot of respite in an arduous part of my journey. I'd been in touch with Leslie ahead of time and arranged to stop, charge my camera batteries, and perhaps enjoy a home-cooked meal.

Ray used to guide canoe trips, and we talked about my NFCT thru-paddle and the adventures of the past week. He thought I'd made the right decision, walking up the Caucomgomoc Stream rapids. Luckily, the water hadn't been too high. I couldn't imagine accomplishing that feat in the spring. According to Ray, the elusive campsite had been in an area of braided islands, perhaps hidden by the one where I'd met the scrambling beaver.

Leslie invited me to explore a couple of the cabins. Their charming rustic decor was perfected in the lodge. Mike Yencha had a friend who had bought a lot of the sporting memorabilia that covered the walls. He would bring it all up, and they would agree on a price, which would then be deducted from the cost of his annual bear hunt. Old signs and framed magazine covers showed wool-and-flannel-clad hunters calling moose, flushing grouse, or sitting by roaring campfires near their upturned canoes. Had any of the colorful old fishing lures really caught the huge fish that adorned the crowded walls? Snowshoes and ice tongs, lanterns and decoys, all were reminders of a way of life still lived out in the Allagash today.

Ray and Leslie would love to play a larger role in the journeys of NFCT thru-paddlers, providing them with frozen meals as they pass by, "so they wouldn't have to live on beans." We knew some of the same people. In 2016, the Allagash Wilderness Waterway marked its 50th anniversary with a July celebration at Churchill Dam. Ray met thru-paddlers Mary Duk and Susan Storch walking a logging road en route to Chamberlain Lake and alerted them to the upcoming event, which would include bateaux rides, tours of the boarding house, blacksmith demonstrations, and a bean hole supper.

"I asked them if they wanted a lift, but they declined. That turned out well for them, as they went by me as I was repairing my truck, which broke down about a mile after I saw them."

At the tramway carry into Eagle Lake, he also told Gabrielle Mutel, Brice Bognet, and their four-year-old son, Malo, about the festivities. The young French family had come to the United States for a few years, while Brice worked as a researcher at the University of Connecticut. They had first thru-paddled the trail in 2015 and were returning that year to do it again.

An article by Jessica Potila in Fort Kent's *Fiddlehead Focus* described the small waterproof bag that Gabrielle, a costume designer, sewed for her young son to carry. In it was "an American flag, a pencil sharpener and a water-resistant notebook in which he colored many pictures of their canoe trail journey."

"And also, this is very important," Gabrielle added, "sprinkles for when we find ice cream."

Loon Lodge currently provides a shuttle service for paddlers. I thought long and hard about having Ray drive me over the first two miles of the long three-mile portage to Allagash Lake, to where a locked gate prohibits further vehicle access. I'd done the NFCT on my own, though, without shuttles, and it seemed wrong to take a ride now.

Up north, one often feels a swift connection with people, as well as the environment. In the photo I snapped of Ray and Leslie, their smiles shine right through to their eyes. Perhaps because of their gray hair and comfortable work clothes, both look capable of dealing cheerfully with the whims of nature and guest. Leslie proclaimed Ray to be "handy with systems," and my breakfast of fried eggs, sausage, juice, and toast was a testament to her talents in the kitchen. Even the sausage tasted homemade.

Ray printed out the latest weather forecast, and Leslie quietly handed me a bag of homemade cookies. We chatted for a while about what it's like to come home from a canoe trip. How you miss the freedom and movement of the river, and how it pulls you back. Somehow, it was almost lunchtime when I left the lodge for the long portage to Allagash Lake.

The Allagash Carry begins at a pair of campsites on the north shore of Round Pond. When I arrived, there was no one around. Gear was spread everywhere, though—tents set up and sleeping bags and clothing drying in the sun. I recognized some of it. The Pine Island campers must be somewhere ahead, portaging their canoes. I began to tie in my paddles and portage yoke, preparing to follow them.

Just then, I heard a vehicle approaching. A pickup truck with an overhead canoe rack pulled up beside me. The driver, Nicky, hopped out with a friendly hello, wondering if I had seen anyone else. He was from Pine Island, there for a resupply. He'd had a flat tire coming in, at the Telos Gate, which had made him late. He'd expected to be moving the campers' canoes, two at a time, as far as the locked gate. Now they had evidently started the carry, and he was going to drive up the road and find them.

I couldn't resist and hoped I wouldn't regret it later.

"If you're going anyway, would you mind carrying my gear, while I carry my canoe?"

"Let's put your canoe up there, too," he offered. "If will only take a minute."

I had to decide, quickly. Feeling more than a little guilty, I piled my paddles and dry bags in the back. Nicky had the canoe secured in not much more than a minute, and we started off down the road.

Soon, we saw the first of the campers. As we passed them, Nicky offered encouragement, but didn't stop. When we caught up to the leaders, he explained about the flat and told them he'd be right back. Now I felt bad, because he still insisted on delivering me to the gate. The condition of the road grew worse. Huge holes gaped across its width, and the truck sank reluctantly into them, then powered up and out.

"Are you sure you really want to drive through this? You could drop me off here."

"Oh, I was thinking I would have to come in here three times.

The truck will be fine. And it's good for those boys to carry the canoes."

As we chatted, I discovered, surprisingly, that Nicky was a kindergarten teacher when he wasn't resupplying campers. I guessed that he was not long out of college. From him, I learned that the boys had been taking canoe trips together for years, gradually gaining experience. For them, this expedition was the culmination of years of ever longer adventures.

At the gate, I thanked Nicky for his kindness and generosity. He had probably saved me from dragging into camp, exhausted, at the edge of dark. Instead, by two in the afternoon, I was a half-mile from Allagash Lake. The walking had been a dream, down a wide and shaded woods road, dry and soft underfoot. I stopped to rest, lying down against a dry bag and my boat. My eyes even drifted closed for a time. I knew that taking the ride had been the right decision.

Not far from there, the road made a turn to the left, and a footpath went off to the right. The path was marked with a sign reading "Carry Trail," but several people had told me that it was best to go left. The road would take me down to the ranger station, right on the lake.

Bob Johnston, a retired cartographer and geologist, was the ranger on Allagash Lake that summer. This is the most remote of the waterway assignments, and he loves it. After thirty-seven years with the Maine Geological Survey, he became an Allagash ranger, working nine days on, then five days off. I found him out of uniform, in a gray T-shirt and old khaki pants, repairing a canoe out in the sunny yard.

"Would you like some tea?" Bob asked, after checking my paperwork.

The tea came with a stack of chocolate chip cookies—it must have been cookie day! We talked, and I discovered that Bob is on the boards of both the Friends of Baxter State Park and the Maine Chapter of the International Appalachian Trail. He had even helped to build several lean-tos in the national monument.

Like all the rangers, Bob can tell you who is traveling through, where they're camped, and even the sights to see. I told him about the group coming in behind me, and we decided that the Ice Cave campsite would be my home that night.

The Allagash Ice Cave, located along the lake's northwest shore, is the longest talus or fissure cave in New England. According to the

Allagash Ranger Bob Johnston encouraged me to climb the fire tower trail

Maine Geological Survey, "Talus or fissure caves are typically found in various types of granite and are caused by large slabs of rock and boulders which have shifted as a result of slides and collapses." There was no way I'd pass by without exploring this one.

"You have to climb Allagash Mountain, too. The view from up there is incredible."

There was a fire tower at the top, and I had been hoping to have time to get up there. The boys began to straggle in as I set off. The trail began right behind the ranger station. It passed through low, damp woods, then started to climb steeply. After a mile of walking and a gain of about 750 feet, I left the forest behind for the windswept summit, at an elevation of 1,807 feet.

A loud whoosh made me jump. With a rush of powerful wings, a group of vultures launched from the rocky ledges. The sky behind them was a deep unbroken blue, and they rode the winds, circling ever higher. The fire tower, a small square building, half weathered shingles and half windows, perched atop long spindly metal legs. The top of the tower frame was anchored with guy wires to the solid rock on which it stood.

Heights don't bother me, and I started up the metal ladder without hesitating. I climbed cautiously, counting twenty rungs, clinging tightly as the wind whipped around me. Below me, the ground receded, until I could reach up and touch the floor of the little room. This was the tricky part. To open the triangular hatch, I would have to let go with one hand. I pushed, needing some force to flip it open. That process was a little scary.

The view was glorious. There was the map I'd studied, come to life. The world spread out below me, the air crystal clear. Sun glinted on Allagash Lake, stretching off to the north. I could trace the route I'd follow from point to point along the west shore toward the Ice Cave campsite. Behind me, to the south, were the sandier shores of Caucomgomoc Lake.

Back on the ground, I picked ripe blueberries, which hung heavy on the bushes, and lingered at the top a little longer. The climb down went more quickly. By then, the campers had finished their portage and were heading out across the lake. Bob kindly filled my bottles with water he'd brought from home and waved good-bye.

Properly equipped with headlamp at the entrance to the Allagash ice cave

The shadows were lengthening as I glided along the rocky western shore of the lake. Near a small island, a couple in a canoe wielded fly rods with well-practiced ease and grace. They'd had some luck fishing this week but would be leaving in the morning. They seemed surprised to learn that I was traveling solo, not with the group of red canoes that had just gone by.

It was four miles to the two campsites near the cave. In the last of the afternoon sun, I swam in the far cove before setting up camp where the morning sun would find me. That evening, the harsh squawking of a multitude of gulls went on for hours, something I'd never before heard up north. Much later, in deep darkness, came a full serenade of loons, their haunting music on a plane far above the uproar of the gulls.

I slept buried in the sleeping bag hood until full light and woke in the morning, excited to explore the cave. The day before, Bob had showed us a map of the underground passages, more extensive than I'd pictured. From camp, it was a quarter mile walk to the main entrance. The roughly rectangular opening, the size of an ordinary door, yawned pitch black. Beyond, I could see a rocky passage dropping down into the earth. I took one look and thought, *I need my headlamp, of course!*

After a round trip back to camp for a light, I stood hesitating before the opening. Bob had told us yesterday that if someone got hurt or lost inside, the rangers were not allowed to attempt a rescue. I thought perhaps that was just a warning to make would-be spelunkers more cautious, but it certainly made me think. *If I fell, how would I call for help?* The SPOT would not work underground.

I set the SPOT on a stump outside and turned on my headlamp. With a deep breath, I entered the cave. A clear passage led ahead and down. There were rocks to cling to and, at first, the ground was dry.

Before long, I began to descend more sharply. I was wearing my Teva sandals, which had better traction than my old river shoes. I hadn't gone far when the glimmer of my headlamp began to reflect off rocks dripping with water. Then I slipped, sliding downward, my fingers struggling to grip the slimy surface.

In a way, it was beautiful. The grays and orange-browns of the crystallized granite, shiny in the eternal wetness, made me want to see more. But my feet could not get a grip on the slippery rock. As I looked up, the entrance was just a tiny sliver of light high above. To descend any further would be committing myself to what looked like a drop down into impenetrable darkness. It was just too risky.

I would probably have been fine, but I barely went out of sight of that window on a safe and sunny world, where birds sang and there was blue and green and gold.

How I would have loved to explore, with a group of people, proper gear, and a sturdy pair of boots. Reluctantly, I climbed back up. There was so much I hadn't seen. On Bob's map, there were many interconnected passages, forming several levels, some quite narrow and challenging.

Deep in the cave, ice sometimes lingers well into summer. In *Allagash: A Journey Through Time on Maine's Legendary Wilderness Waterway*, Master Maine Guide Gil Gilpatrick writes, "I never really believed that there was ice to be found there all summer long. In my first visit my skepticism was reinforced as I looked at the shiny, wet fungus that grows on the cave walls—it looks very much like ice in the glare of a flashlight beam. For many years I was smug in the knowledge that I was correct about the source of the name. But then one day in late July my theory was shattered. I watched a young camper come down the trail with a chunk of ice the size of a large bucket. It could only have come from one of the caves."

Gilpatrick had explored further than I had, following the passage steeply downward for twenty or thirty feet to a large chamber. "Large is relative, but here it means there is room for several people to stand around and talk. I have never ventured beyond this point. On the way down to the chamber, there is a place where you have to lie on your back and slide through a narrow opening. As I did this on one occasion, I looked at the roof of the cave, about six inches above my face, and there was a bat hanging there. He was apparently used to these interruptions of his daily sleep time, because he was still there on my way out."

Today, the bats living in Allagash Lake's ice caves face a serious threat, one that annually closes the caves to visitors from October 1 through April 30. These are the months when bats hibernate. In Maine, there are at least three hibernacula—caves or mines where colonies of bats hibernate—and all of them have been infected by white-nose syndrome. This fungal disease is named for the white fuzzy growth that often appears on the noses, wings, and other hairless parts of infected bats.

The fungus that causes the disease, *Pseudogymnoascus destrucans*, is native to Europe and Asia, where bats seem to have natural resistance to the disease. In North America, the story is much sadder. White-nose syndrome, first documented in New York in 2006, reached Maine five years later. The Maine Department of Inland Fisheries and Wildlife has been monitoring bat populations in the Allagash ice caves since the mid-1990s, prior to the arrival of the disease.

"We have seen an approximately 95 percent decline in little brown and northern long-eared bats hibernating in that cave since WNS hit," reports Shevenell Webb, MDIFW biologist. "These are similar to population declines found in other northeastern states for these species. Not all individuals show signs of WNS, so there is a bright side."

Some North American bats aren't vulnerable to white-nose syndrome. Species that migrate to warmer climates are not exposed to the fungus during hibernation. Others seem to have a natural immunity to the disease. Unfortunately, five of Maine's eight bat species hibernate—the big brown bat, little brown bat, northern long-eared bat, eastern small-footed bat, and tri-colored bat—and all have experienced mortality as a result of WNS.

"During hibernation," explains the MDIFW website, "metabolic activities are greatly reduced. A bat's normal body temperature of around 100 degrees F. is reduced to just one or two degrees higher than that of the hibernaculum, and the heart rate slows to only one beat every four or five seconds. A hibernating bat can thus survive on only a few grams of stored fat during the five- to six-month hibernation period."

The deadly mechanism of white-nose syndrome impacts that delicate balance. According to the US Fish and Wildlife Service, the fungus "attacks and grows on bats while they are in an inactive state of hibernation. The fungus damages skin so much that bats warm up and become active, wasting energy they need to make it through the winter...bats with WNS act strangely during cold winter months, including flying outside during the day."

By closing caves during the winter hibernation period, there is less chance of disturbing bats or transmitting the fungus to other regions. The MDIFW reports that "a single disturbance probably costs a bat as much energy as it would normally expend in two to three weeks of hibernation."

Beyond avoiding caves in winter, there are other ways to help the population rebound. At times, bats hibernate in structures like barns or attics and shouldn't be disturbed after late September. Female bats usually give birth in late spring, to just one pup, which doesn't fly for the first month.

"If you have bats roosting in domestic structures, allow them to rear their pups and exit the structure at the end of the summer before closing off any entrance holes," advises the MDIFW website. There are pages of information there on bat-friendly construction and the installation of bat houses, which are frequently used by Maine's little brown bat and big brown bat.

Sometimes it's only when we are about to lose something that we begin to fully appreciate its value. A nursing little brown bat consumes her body weight in insects every summer night, eating mosquitoes, flies, moths, and beetles. To date, over one million of the Northeast's little brown bats have died as a result of this deadly disease.

CHAPTER 5

JUST ONE MORE

The most remarkable piece of construction of this whole railroad project was the trestle across Allagash Stream at the northern end of Chamberlain Lake…it was a masterpiece of backwoods engineering.

—**Gil Gilpatrick,** *Allagash: A Journey Through Time on Maine's Legendary Wilderness Waterway*

As I left camp, I could see a line of red canoes coming across Allagash Lake, headed straight for the ice caves. I was sure the adventurous campers would go farther into the caves than I had.

The previous evening's raucous clamor was fresh in my mind. I knew where it had originated, a rocky island to the north. Despite a brisk wind and sizable waves, I altered course to pass close by. The sheer number of birds was intimidating. They were herring gulls, the adults with white heads and bodies, gray backs, and black-tipped wings. Common terns also nest on Allagash Lake, and I had seen a few yesterday, but there were none here. The gulls, many with the darker coloration of the immature, soared and wheeled above me. From the whirling cloud, some dove, squawking in outrage.

As I neared the small nesting island, it had the feel of a citadel. A couple of hardy birch clung to the bare craggy rock, along with the tall skeleton of a long-dead tree. Droppings ran like white paint down the sides of every rock. Strong waves hurtled me past, but not quickly enough for the gulls, who escorted me away like bouncers.

With the wind's help, I flew across the northeast corner of the

lake, surfing along on the crests of the waves. The Outlet campsite had a broad, beautiful view down the lake. Straight before me,
Allagash Mountain rose against a bank of white clouds, with substance to them. Above them, thin, wispy clouds floated in the azure
sky. I could just make out the tiny fire tower. The sun was shining,
and I had made it to Allagash Stream, which would bring me to
Chamberlain Lake and familiar waters.

I wandered barefoot on the beach, munching trail mix. Squinting,
I could just make out the tiny shape of a boat, which slowly grew
larger—the welcome sight of Bob, the Allagash ranger, puttering toward me in his skiff. His was the only motor allowed on the remote
lake, another of its fine attributes. To have arrived here, one must have
contributed some effort, on foot or by canoe. Float planes are not allowed on Allagash Lake. Anyone dropped off by plane at Johnson
Pond or Chamberlain Lake would then have to paddle in, arriving
from upstream or downstream along Allagash Stream.

We chatted, and then Bob saw me off, making sure I was wearing socks. I had learned years ago that one can get blisters just as easily in the river as on a mountain trail. Usually I wore thin polypro-
pylene sock liners designed for hiking under my Chaco river sandals.

Bob was somewhat reassuring about conditions on Allagash
Stream. "You'll be able to paddle the deadwaters, but you'll defi-
nitely be doing plenty of walking, especially at the beginning. There's
a huge tree down about a mile in. The deadwaters are after that. You'll
do fine."

I started around noon, after lifting over the remains of an old
log-driving dam. For some reason, this wild place felt beyond the
realm of the logging empire, but I guess it wasn't. According to the
AMC river guide, it was 2.75 miles to Little Round Pond, through
continuous Class I rapids and quick water. Optimistically, I was hoping that there would be enough water to stay in the boat much of
the time.

Until I reached Bob's huge dead tree, though, the stream was
mostly too bony to paddle. I love that term, *bony*, which is so descriptive of these rocky streams when the water is low. Occasionally, I
could paddle a short distance before hopping out once more. I redis-
covered the technique of walking behind the boat, guiding it along in

front of me, which felt safer on the slick rocks. Progress was slow, and, by one o'clock, when I stopped for lunch, I had come less than a mile in more than an hour.

I found the dead tree, and paddled gingerly underneath, where someone had sawn off some of the branches. Soon, the character of the stream began to mellow. The water gradually deepened, and the rocks gave way to sandy banks, with shrubby alder stretching out over the water.

From there, I paddled most of the way to Little Round Pond, only hopping out three times at shallow spots. Once, I heard a sound like rapids ahead, the unmistakable cascade of dropping water. It was a large beaver dam, new and as neatly constructed as any I had seen. These master engineers never cease to impress me with their accomplishments. The water was so deep above the dam that I couldn't stand in the stream but balanced atop the tightly woven logs to work my canoe up and over.

When the water of the pond opened out before me, I couldn't help grinning. It was quite shallow and only a half-mile across, but it was a milestone. The upper section of Allagash Stream was behind me, and tonight I would camp beside Little Allagash Falls, just across the pond.

Near the spot where Allagash Stream exited the pond, I discovered a clump of white water lilies, the first of the trip. The fragrant water lily is one of Maine's showiest native aquatic species, gorgeous enough to grace Monet's garden at Giverny. The round floating leaf has a wedge-shaped notch that penetrates almost to its center. The classical flower, several inches in diameter, has a cluster of pure white pointed petals around a bright-yellow bunch of stamens. The flowers, which open in early morning and close by late afternoon, are indeed delicately fragrant.

Following Bob's advice, I paddled to the second campsite to take out. From there, the 150-yard portage trail went up through the second and third campsites to the put-in below the falls. There, I flipped my canoe upside down over my boating gear, well up from the stream. Little Allagash Falls drops twenty feet over an outcropping of smooth dark Seboomook slate. Under glowering clouds, I took a quick look and hurried back to set up camp.

All evening it drizzled. I tried making a campfire, then decided to start the book of O. Henry short stories I had brought along. As the drizzle turned to rain, there was satisfaction in knowing that everything was dry and stowed. I like to bring as much of my gear as I can inside the tent, including my PFD, which makes a great pillow for reading. After cooking chicken and pasta under the shelter of the tent vestibule, I turned in for the night.

The forecast was for days of wet weather ahead, and I woke to a light and steady rain. My body was already aching, so I took an Aleve before rereading the description of the 2.25 miles of Allagash Stream ahead. The rain would help, as I faced several Class II rapids within the generally Class I whitewater. In a quarter mile, there would be two ledges and then a short rapid under a bridge. The first ledge could be avoided by going to the right of a midstream island.

Sometimes, though, knowing what's ahead can be more confusing than not knowing. I had already been in and out of the canoe several times and carried past two exposed ledges, not runnable at this low water level, when I came to the first spot even mentioned in the guide. There was the island and a way around to the right, if you walked. I stepped cautiously on rounded rocks green with algae, following the green and red scrapes of paint from those who'd gone before.

There, on that small island, I discovered a gorgeous flower—the lesser purple fringed bog orchid. The upper part of each stem was covered with buds, perhaps thirty on each, above several alternate elongated leaves. The lower buds had opened to reveal delicate, fringed pale-lavender flowers, with the promise of many more unopened buds above. This orchid, pollinated by moths and butterflies, can be found in wetlands across New England, but I did not remember having seen it before.

These midstream islands were worlds unto their own, where tall lush grasses were dotted with the colors of summer. Here, a clump of the exquisite little orchids was surrounded by yellow swamp candle, pink Joe Pye weed, and an abundance of white-flowering elderberry. This island garden grew, unencumbered by shade, except for a couple of grandfatherly northern white cedar.

Soon, I arrived at the second major ledge and lifted over it on river left, as instructed. This little stream was turning out to be fun. I threaded my way through simple rapids, often seeing only one line where the canoe would have enough water to sneak through. Sometimes the pull of the current helped guide me to the deepest channel. Later, in my journal, I wrote, *I liked today's challenge—reading the river, and all the times I chose right and wiggled my way down.*

Hints of brightness began to lighten the day, and the rain turned to a fine mist.

About a mile from the start, I came to the logging road bridge. I pulled over, got out, and was climbing the bank when I saw a ranger walking toward me from his parked truck. Ben was one of two Allagash rangers at Chamberlain Bridge, where I would be meeting my parents in two days.

"I'm walking in, to surprise Bob," he explained. Bob had told me that he was going to be doing some work at the Little Allagash Falls campsites that morning.

I told Ben about my journey and asked which of the campsites on the upper part of Chamberlain Lake were the most attractive.

"Just stay on the west shore," he answered. "All of the sites from Lost Spring down are nice."

Then he continued, "I just opened Telos Dam. We're dropping the level of Chamberlain one foot, seven inches to do some work on Lock Dam. Right now, it's at 236 cfs. That should help you out."

That was excellent news, as water levels in both Telos Cut and Webster Stream would benefit.

"Thanks! That reminds me," I asked. "Do you ever open the dam just to release extra water for paddlers, especially if you have a group coming through?"

Ben replied that they didn't, despite what I'd heard from an experienced paddler who had been through there before. Luckily, I had just happened along at a good time.

The rest of Allagash Stream went more quickly. I was puzzled by several mounds of pebbles, a foot or two in length, protruding from the stream. Later, Bob told me they were "chub fish" nests, exposed by the low water levels. The fallfish (*Semotilus corporalis*), or "chub," is one of the state's largest native minnows. Darker above, its thick body is covered with prominent shiny, metallic looking silver scales.

Anglers in pursuit of trout or salmon commonly catch fallfish from four to eight inches in length in Maine lakes and streams. However, the fish is known to attain lengths approaching two feet.

In the spring, the male makes a nest in the sand and gravel bed of a stream, carrying stones in his mouth. After the female spawns, the male covers the nest with more gravel, creating a mound. According to the website of the New Hampshire Fish and Game Department, "spawning is communal, although usually initiated by the nest builder, with a number of females and surrounding males using a single nest."

There is always something new to learn.

Near its end, Allagash Stream widens considerably before flowing into the lake. In the water ahead, I could make out five large heaps of stone on the left marching toward a wavering line of broken, weathered wooden pilings on the right. Together, they traced the line of the historic Eagle Lake & West Branch Railroad, where it had once crossed Allagash Stream on a fifteen-hundred-foot wooden trestle.

The railroad, in operation from 1927 to 1933, carried railcars of pulpwood for thirteen miles, from Eagle Lake to Umbazooksus Lake. From there, the logs were floated down Chesuncook Lake to the Great Northern Paper Company mill on the West Branch, just above where it joined the East Branch. Fully loaded, a ninety- or hundred-ton steam locomotive would pull a dozen metal railcars, each holding twelve and a half cords of pulpwood, across this thin trestle, ten feet above the water.

The tracks were still there. From the left, they ran along the top of the stone piles, which I could now see were surrounded by timber cribbing. In the center, where the water was deepest, the tracks disappeared into the depths before rising again to twist and turn among the pilings like a crazy roller coaster. It felt eerie to paddle over them near the spot where they dove into the dark water.

A half-mile more, and I was out on the lake. Instantly, the wind met me, strong from the southeast. In the Allagash region, the prevailing winds, or those you would typically find, blow from the northwest, giving those going down the lake a helpful push. Unfortunately,

Remnants of the 1500-foot West Branch & Eagle Lake Railroad trestle

the wind today was blowing in the opposite direction. Paddling down the west shore, I went a couple of miles, arriving at the Lost Spring campsite around three in the afternoon.

The waves crashing up on shore made the decision for me. I would stop there for the night. Windbound after just five hours of travel, I was nonetheless grateful to be safely on Chamberlain. The sun wandered in and out, and a mother merganser with three young offspring bounced by. I finished my camp chores and stretched out against a comfortable rock.

It was time to rest, to simply sit, to reflect and write—and drink hot cider with rum.

The beach is crafted of thin, smooth pebbles, worn by the waves to a surprising softness. The effect is comfortable for sitting. In the warm breeze, I wear my cotton T-shirt, and there are no bugs. Here is the coming together of countless bits of rock, no two shapes, colors, or stories the same. I have the history of the earth to sit on. It feels as though there could be no one else anywhere in this "lonely land." The crash of waves, the alert huddle of a red squirrel on a nearby bough—this is my company. I look to the skies, or the discovery of a flower, for my conversation. This is where we must go to remember who we are, and draw closer to God, who made us to feel this oneness with our world.

For dinner, I cooked some dehydrated baked beans my father had mixed up for me, with the last of the bacon pieces. They were delicious. On these huge lakes, it's early to bed, early to rise.

I was up and out on the water the next morning soon after five. I paddled with the strength of early morning, along a rocky shoreline. I could tell the water level was down, and grass filled the wide gap between forest and shore. Two mergansers flew before me, standing as stalwart sentinels on large rocks until I got close, then moving on. The shaggy crests on their copper heads seemed to blow back as the wind came up. Finally, they gave up and retreated to the other side of the lake. The drumming of a woodpecker came from the forest, and a spotted sandpiper darted along the shore, bobbing his tail in constant motion as he searched for insects.

Biting flies found the tender spots on my feet and behind my knees, and I twitched, too.

By eight o'clock, I had come five miles, a respectable distance considering the wind was again in my face. *I'd rather have the head-wind and sun than tailwind and rain.* A half hour later, it was rougher, and conditions were rapidly deteriorating. At Donnelly Point, a beautiful open campsite looking south down the lake, I stopped to rest. I pulled out my map and spread it out, with my water bottle to keep it from blowing away.

Not far ahead along the west shore was the spot where Mud Brook flowed from Mud Pond into Chamberlain. Twice before, I had come into the Allagash that way, through an ancient portage route called Mud Pond Carry. Both times I had collapsed in sheer exhaustion at the first campsite I came to, called Mud Brook, about a mile south of Donnelly Point.

Mud Pond Carry, a rite of passage for thru-paddlers, may be the worst portage on the Northern Forest Canoe Trail. It's tough, a 1.8-mile slog through a running stream or ankle-deep mud that hides slick rocks and treacherous logs. Slithering under and over downed trees, pursued by black flies, I had survived it in 2011 and again in 2015.

Now I'd come into the Allagash another way. From the point where I'd turned up Caucomgomoc Stream five days earlier, it was only a dozen miles to this spot. Thru-paddlers typically cross the north end of Chesuncook Lake, then follow Umbazooksus Stream to Umbazooksus Lake and the rock cairn marking the start of the carry. Looking at the map, I decided that Mud Pond Carry might be horrendous, but it was also a lot shorter and simpler than the route I'd just followed.

I ended up spending the day at Donnelly Point. First, I tried to go on. After a tricky launching, I had only gone a short way when powerful gusts brought me to a standstill, then began to turn the boat. I wasn't in control anymore, and it felt dangerous, so I turned back.

Being windbound is a combination of freedom and frustration. For a time, planned schedules must be set aside, and you can choose your activity. At the same time, hours or days are evaporating without any forward progress. In my case, I needed to be at the south end of Chamberlain Lake, about nine miles away, by noon tomorrow. For now, though, there was nothing I could do about it.

In the afternoon, I sat in the shade of an ancient white pine and caught up on my journaling.

All day, tongues of white have rolled and frolicked as far as I can see. Once, a diving duck, thin and agile, rode the waves right off my little beach, then dove and disappeared. This campsite's red squirrel doesn't scold but has snuck up to me three times while I keep watch over the water. I've eaten and drunk, swum and sunbathed, napped and read and written. My exploring didn't lead to any berries. Last night there was an opening, probably the old railroad grade, behind camp, loaded with raspberries.

Around four in the afternoon, I was ready to try again. I fought my way toward the Mud Brook campsite, the one I'd been so thankful to reach after completing the carry in years past. The gusts continued to come in spurts. I could paddle, and then the force would bring me to a standstill. Once, when I paused to look around, a canoe had appeared along the shore behind me like a mirage. Where it came from or where it went afterward, I do not know. At last, I pulled into the campsite, safe for now.

To continue, I would have to cross in front of the entrance into the little pond that lies at the mouth of Mud Brook. On the map, it looks narrow and insignificant. That afternoon, though, large waves were building on the pond, then funneling through the narrow channel and hurtling toward the main part of the lake. I thought of stopping, but after all that resting, I felt fresh and wanted to go on. *Just one more campsite to the south*, I told myself.

Committing myself to the rolling waves, I angled safely through and followed the shore deep into the next cove. When at last I could turn with the wind at my back, I joyfully rode the waves out of the cove, straight to the next campsite, called Gravel Beach. Chunk by chunk, my rendezvous was getting closer. Along this sheltered shore, I found calmer water and decided to go on. *Just one more campsite*, I said again.

At Rocky Cove, three miles farther south, the site was shaded by woods that gathered close around the picnic table. The prospect of camping there did not appeal to me. *Just one more*, I thought. By then, it was six o'clock. The next site was Ledge Point, high on a bluff, a fabulous place to stay.

Where the map showed two sites, though, there turned out to be just one. As I paddled closer, bright spots of color became boys in bathing suits, shouting to each over as they scrambled over the rocky cliffs. Behind them, a tidy camp was filled with tents. It was a group from Damariscotta Lake's Camp Kieve, where I'd often gone with school groups. Their leader volunteered to share the space.

"You can have the picnic table," he generously offered, but I decided to keep going.

Just one more. I was feeling the long day now, running on willpower and the calories from all that midday food I'd eaten. Along this more exposed shore, the wind was strong in my face again. At last, I saw the point marking the entrance to the Thoroughfare, the short, narrow neck that led to Chamberlain Bridge and the ranger station. Victory! Tomorrow, it would be just a quick paddle to meet my parents.

The Boy Scout campsite is huge, meant to accommodate large groups beginning the Allagash. I had it all to myself. I perched my tent near the edge of a high bank, looking out at the sunset sky. Above me, the white moon was almost full. I felt a contentment beyond words.

After a restful morning in camp, I paddled the short distance to the Chamberlain Bridge ranger station. There, the posted forecast was for continued south winds, nine to thirteen mph, with gusts to twenty-four. More of the same, along with heavy rain, was predicted for the following day. Jay was the ranger on duty that day. Continuing the Allagash tradition of fine hospitality, he made me tea while we visited.

My faithful support team arrived just before noon, bringing food, supplies, maps for the upcoming sections, and even clean clothes. Like a touch of home, Mom had brought hard-boiled eggs and the cheese, fruit, and vegetables that I'd had on my list. It was so good to sit in the sun and pour out the stories of my adventures so far.

The boat landing was a busy place that morning. A different Pine Island group pulled up and quickly began loading their canoes for a six-day trip down the Allagash. Then Will Hackett, a friend from Kieve's leadership school, arrived to resupply the campers that I'd met the day before. After reaching the end of the Allagash River, they would continue down the St. John River to take out in St. Francis. The Northern Forest Canoe Trail went that way, as did most Allagash visitors.

Today, they would all have the wind at their backs. I would not.

To the south, lay Telos, the southernmost of the Allagash lakes and new territory for me.

Only in 1857 did Thoreau get as far north as the Allagash. His party reached Chamberlain Lake via the Mud Pond Carry route, then crossed into the southern end of Eagle Lake. From there, he returned to Chamberlain and continued south. The rest of my canoe trip would mirror his, all on waters new to me.

I drank a can of spicy V-8, too heavy to carry along, and double-checked the maps and paperwork. In among the papers I had packed before the trip was something new. The clump of stapled pages was entitled *Maverick and Goose Go for a Paddle: Webster Brook and the East Branch of the Penobscot.* The cover sported a photo of actors Anthony Edwards, "Goose," and Tom Cruise, "Maverick," from the movie *Top Gun.*

Just weeks before, two brave souls had borrowed the names of fictional fighter pilots and taken to the water in search of adventure. To tell their story, we must jump back in time.

It had been seventeen days since I'd hefted the weight of a moderately heavy backpack and started down a dusty, sunbaked logging road deep within the national monument. My odyssey had begun more slowly, on foot and far from the water. Ascending mountain peaks, the world had dropped away into a thousand shades of green, rising and falling in waves broken only by shining lakes and the winding ribbon of river. Descending to the river shore, I had scouted some of the most challenging rapids and portages that I would later encounter. Near the end of the hike, at the last rapid, a surprise awaited.

In the way of wilderness serendipity, which often delivers the most improbable of gifts, it was there that I met the paddlers known within these pages as "Goose" and "Maverick."

PART II

THE HIKE

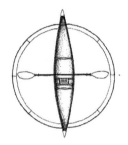

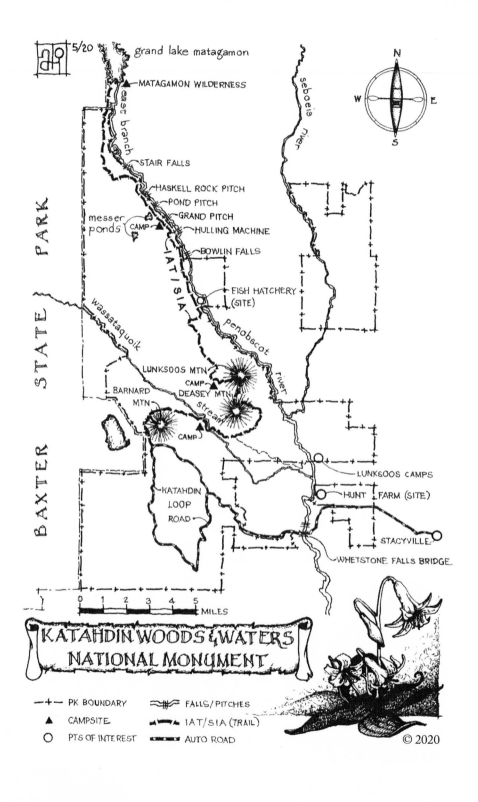

KATAHDIN WOODS & WATERS
NATIONAL MONUMENT

CHAPTER 6

THE START OF A LONG WALK

Few people know how to take a walk. The qualifications are
endurance, plain clothes, old shoes, an eye for nature, good humor,
vast curiosity, good speech, good silence and nothing too much.

—Ralph Waldo Emerson

The bright-pink, spiky blooms of fireweed matched the color of Mom's shirt as she smiled for the photo. She stood by a long sign board at a viewpoint in Katahdin Woods and Waters National Monument. Behind her, just nine miles away, towered Katahdin, its sculpted ridges and basins clearly visible on this fine sunny day. Dad had already driven us about halfway around the monument's Loop Road toward the spot where my backpacking adventure would begin.

The scene at the overlook was what you would expect and, then again, it wasn't.

The raw material to work with was stunning. To the left, Millinocket Lake sparkled in the foreground, in front of no fewer than eleven mountain peaks, ranging in elevation from Hammond Ridge at 1,085 feet to Big Spencer Mountain at 3,206 feet. To the right, the view was dominated by Katahdin, dwarfing the others. Its summit capped out at an impressive 5,267 feet. Large boulders rimmed the parking area, and tables sat waiting for picnickers.

Surprisingly, the two sign boards at this popular viewpoint were handmade, constructed in 2014 by Joy Allen McEwen of nearby Millinocket. The wood-burned diagrams of the landscape features were a work of art more distinctive than any of the hundreds of National Park Service interpretive signs I'd seen in my life. So far, my impression of Katahdin Woods and Waters could be summed up by those finely crafted signs. This was a new place, brimming with possibility, still unfolding, and warmly welcoming in an amateur, homespun way.

For years, there had been plenty of opposition to federal management of these lands. Maine's governor, Paul LePage, who had pushed for the establishment of a state park instead, had prohibited the posting of any highway signage directing visitors to the monument. On the drive in, we'd even passed several signs still reading, "This Bridge Owner Says National Park No." They hearkened back to the time when a bona fide national park had been under consideration.

Of course, instead of a national park, Katahdin Woods and Waters National Monument had been created almost two years earlier. Now, it seemed, this 87,563-acre gem was here to stay, although there were no park rangers, no entrance fees, and the infrastructure was still in flux.

The small town of Stacyville, Maine has long been a jumping off point for exploring the Katahdin region. In Stacyville, just five miles along State Route 11 from Interstate 95, we turned right onto Swift Brook Road. Following the rugged gravel road, we drove seven miles to a narrow wood-planked bridge whose importance only gradually dawned on me.

This was my first look at the East Branch of the Penobscot River. If all went well, a few weeks from now my canoe would glide around the bend above and face the high rocky ledges, narrow rapids, and sandbar upon which I now looked down. This was Whetstone Falls, hopefully runnable, just outside the monument boundary and some nine miles above where I planned to finish at Grindstone Falls.

At the monument boundary, an official looking dark-brown sign with white letters announced, "ENTERING KATAHDIN WOODS & WATERS NATIONAL MONUMENT." My heart thumped with anticipation. We were truly here.

About three miles past the bridge, we reached the Sandbank Stream picnic and camping area, formerly a sand and gravel pit. The vehicle-accessible campsites were more utilitarian than scenic, but the large privy was clean and in mint condition. Another highlight was a freshly constructed informational kiosk, where we found Loop Road interpretive maps, courtesy of the nonprofit organization Friends of Katahdin Woods and Waters. This group was also in the process of publishing a high-quality, waterproof trail map that I would discover later, while doing the canoe portion of my trip.

The seventeen-mile Loop Road varies in width and condition, sometimes sharing busy logging roads. Trucks can come barreling along and always have the right of way. The speed limit of fifteen miles per hour was as fast as we wanted to go on most of it, though we've also driven far worse. Visitors are encouraged to travel the loop clockwise, following mile markers measured from the Sandbank Stream campsites. Miles 6.4 through 9 are one-way in that direction.

Pushed for time, we had to pass up exploring some intriguing habitats mentioned on the map. The monument uses Maine Natural Areas Program (MNAP) guidelines to define natural communities. The mandate of this state-administered program is to "inventory the State's natural areas, including, but not limited to, rare plants, animals, natural communities and ecosystems or other geological, hydrological, natural historical, scenic or other similar features," maintaining a comprehensive database of the results. Using this classification system, at least thirty-seven natural communities have been identified within the monument. Three of these are considered "imperiled" and seven "rare" in Maine.

Along the Loop Road, for example, visitors have access to a *leatherleaf boggy fen* surrounding Lynx Pond, via a short trail from Mile 2.2. This fascinating natural community features classic wetland plants such as Labrador tea, sheep laurel, and leatherleaf, as well as the carnivorous pitcher plant and round-leaved sundew. Both common goldeneye and ring-necked ducks are known to nest there.

Around two, we pulled into the parking area at Mile 11.8. I posed for a photo by the sign marking the start of the International Appalachian Trail (IAT). Squinting into intense sun, hiking poles in hand, I smiled away any trepidation I felt. I urged Mom and Dad to start the long drive home, as I would need to wait while the SPOT

At the very start of the International Appalachian Trail

sent a message before I could get moving. They drove away, somehow leaving me feeling more vulnerable than on the many times they'd left me along a river or lakeshore.

To understand and appreciate the trail ahead will take some imagination.

Picture the world, 390 million years ago. Though things look vastly different, the pieces of land that will one day become Maine are there. The bulk of North America, partly covered by a shallow tropical sea, lies south of the equator. The Atlantic has not yet been born, but for hundreds of millions of years another ocean, the Iapetus, has separated the continent from Eurasia.

The seas of the Devonian Period teem with life. There are brachiopods and trilobites, jointed cephalopods, feathery crinoids, and plain old snails, all of which will someday be found as fossils in Maine's sedimentary rocks. Predatory armored placoderms, the first jawed fish, top the food chain. Lobe-finned fishes, much like the "living fossil" coelacanth, will soon spark an evolutionary chain that will end with the first amphibians.

Insects have appeared, and plant species are exploding, becoming larger and more complex. Soon, the power of photosynthesis will begin to increase the level of oxygen in the atmosphere. In freshwater and brackish marshes lives one of the largest plants on Earth, *Pertica quadrifaria*. Six feet tall, it has rows of branches spiraling up its stem. There are both fertile and sterile branches, the former producing spores and the latter simply forking at the end. This extinct species, first identified in 1968 from a Baxter State Park fossil, could represent an early evolutionary step toward leafed plants. In 1985, *Pertica quadrifaria* was designated Maine's official state fossil.

Beneath the oceans, too, things are changing. Cracks in the sea floor stretch for thousands of miles, dividing Earth's thin crust into vast plates. High on the plates ride continents, slowly, inexorably on the move. Sometimes, molten rock oozes up from the next layer down—the mantle—widening the cracks. Sometimes pieces of the sea floor are dragged down through faults, pulling land masses closer together.

Long before the Devonian, for hundreds of millions of years, the plates had been migrating in this manner. Gradually, the Iapetus Ocean was shrinking, bringing islands and small landmasses from afar and welding them onto the mainland. The study of plate tectonics uses many clues to track these movements: the fossil record, rock types, radioactive dating, and even remnant magnetism, a record within iron-bearing volcanic rocks of their position relative to Earth's magnetic field at the time they formed.

One pioneer in this field of study was United States Geological Survey scientist Robert B. Neuman, who worked extensively within and in an area just north and east of Katahdin Woods and Waters National Monument. If you are fortunate enough to climb to the summit of Sugarloaf Mountain, elevation 1,864 feet, in Township

T5 R7 WELS near Shin Pond, the grand scale of the national monument will unfold before you. This is not the well-known Carrabassett Valley skiing destination, by the way, but an identically named mountain equally famous among geologists, thanks to Neuman's many summers of work there in the 1950s and 1960s.

From the summit of flat-topped Sugarloaf, a breathtaking view sweeps across a valley of unbroken forest, toward the spectacular silhouettes of Katahdin and Traveler Mountain. Spread your arms wide to embrace this gift of an expanse of land unparalleled in the state since the founding of Baxter State Park. Then look closer at the mountain on which you are standing.

On a smaller scale, the outcroppings of this unique mountain reveal a fascinating saga. The foundational bedrock in this area is some of the oldest in Maine. Overlying it are other, younger formations. It was the rock and imbedded fossils of the Shin Brook formation that most captured Neuman's interest. Dating to the Early Ordovician Period, from 485 to 470 million years ago, the Shin Brook formation was composed of a mixture of volcanic ash, sandstone, and breccia— rock containing large angular fragments. Neuman would go on to prove this rock did not originate anywhere near Maine.

In a Maine Geological Survey publication, State Geologist Robert G. Marvinney explains, "In the Shin Brook Formation, Neuman identified fossils at eight localities, with the largest number and greatest variety coming from localities on Sugarloaf. These include six species of brachiopods (similar to modern clams) and several trilobite species. Notably, this locality marked the discovery of the new genus and species, *Platytoechia boucoti*, a thin brachiopod with a finely striated shell. The really fascinating thing to geologists is that the assemblage of fossils in the Shin Brook Formation, as Neuman discovered, are unlike the North American fauna of that time period, and more like the fauna of Ireland. Somehow the tectonic forces at play in the ancestral Atlantic Ocean rafted islands with Celtic fauna to the shore of North America!"

It is not too much of a stretch to say that a climb up Shin Pond's Sugarloaf Mountain, a mere three miles from the monument's Seboeis parcel, is truly a scramble over an ancient Irish island.

Moving toward modern times, and returning to our story of Devonian days, the plates have continued to drift. A catastrophic collision is imminent. The first of several large landmasses is about to strike the North American continent, a process that will continue until the ocean has disappeared and Euramerica is a single landmass. Far in the future, when the continents are once more torn apart, some of this exotic rock will remain, forming much of the coast of Maine.

This collision with the microcontinent of Avalonia doubled the thickness of the crust. The massive weight of the overlying rock forced the lower crust deeper, the heat and pressure changing its very nature. Through this process of metamorphosis came the shales and quartzites, for example, that are found within the monument today. Deep in the crust, other rock melted and was injected into the upper crust, cooling into the impressive granite outcroppings of the Katahdin region. The uplifting of the Appalachian mountain range, which likely once soared as high as the Rockies, began with the Avalonian collision.

Millions more years passed, and the mountains were worn away by erosion. Meanwhile, the continents continued their journeys. Eventually, the supercontinent of Pangaea formed, incorporating all the landmasses we know today. Maine, near its center, had drifted slightly north of the equator, where Ghana is now. Its climate was most likely hot and dry.

The only geological constant, though, is change. Almost two hundred million years ago, Pangaea began to break apart. By then, Maine was at a latitude of 35 degrees north, only ten degrees south of where it is today. Eventually, North America and Eurasia parted company, but along a different seam from where they had merged. The ancient chain of mountains—called the Appalachians in North America, the Caledonides in Europe, and the Atlas Mountains in Morocco—was torn apart, separated by the newly forming Atlantic Ocean. What had been a contiguous range now marched across three continents—eastern North America, including Greenland; western Europe; and northwestern Africa.

Katahdin is one of those mountains, along with the march of her sisters to the south—Mt. Washington, Mt. Rogers, Clingmans Dome, and many more, all the way to the southern end of the Appalachian National Scenic Trail and beyond.

Since Earl Shaffer in 1948, triumphant northbound AT thru-hikers have celebrated summiting Katahdin, finishing their long walks. Although the AT ends there, 2,188 miles from Georgia's Springer Mountain, the venerable chain of mountains meanders on. Where does it go? Where does it end? In the minds of an ever-growing number of dedicated trail builders and indefatigable hikers, the end lies as far away as distant Morocco. These mountains, bound together by their origin over millions of years of geological turmoil, are now bound together in another way. The tale of the trail began around twenty-five years ago.

The vision for an international hiking trail north of Katahdin was announced by gubernatorial candidate Joseph E. Brennan at a press conference in Portland, Maine, on Earth Day, April 22, 1994. Brennan, who had served as the 70th Governor of Maine, was running for re-election against Susan Collins and Angus King. Among his top priorities was to strengthen ties with Maine's Canadian

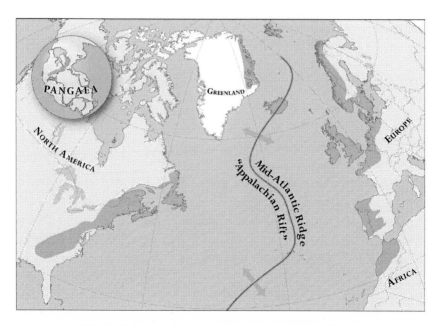

The Appalachian terrane, shown in gray, unites hikers around the Atlantic Ocean (Map by Bill Duffy, Northern Geomantics)

neighbors. He had also encouraged conservationist Dick Anderson, who was working on his campaign, to brainstorm possible environmental initiatives to be announced on Earth Day.

As a wildlife and fisheries biologist, Anderson had a very good working knowledge of New Brunswick and Québec from past projects there. In 1988, for instance, he had flown by helicopter over the Chic-Choc Mountains of the Gaspé with naturalist Don Hudson, while studying caribou habitat and migration patterns as part of a proposed caribou reintroduction plan for Maine. Tracing the spine of the Appalachians, they discussed the similarity of the landscape and ecology to that of their home state.

Years later, the spark of an idea would come to Anderson—the dream of a trail that would foster collaboration with neighboring provinces, boost tourism in communities along the route, encourage environmental stewardship, and highlight the shared geology and ecology that crosses borders worldwide. Don Hudson, too, would stand with Joe Brennan on that historic day and go on to become a strong force in the leadership and expansion of the trail. Hudson currently serves as both the co-chair of the International IAT Council and president of the IAT Maine Chapter, where Anderson is a valuable member of the board of directors.

"Nature knows no boundaries," said Brennan, "I am confident that this narrow trail connecting the special wild places in each of our political jurisdictions will serve as a reminder that the mountains and the rivers and the forests are our real heritage, our common biological and geological bond. They will outlast us all and it is up to us to see that their health and grandeur can be enjoyed by all the generations of mankind that follow us as inhabitants of this special corner of the Earth."

Although Brennan did not win the election, the trail grew and flourished. The goal in the early years was to partner with the provinces of New Brunswick and Québec, to build a trail that would follow the northern Appalachians from Katahdin to Mont Carleton in New Brunswick, then onward to Mont Jacques-Cartier, at the end of the Gaspé Peninsula. They christened it the International Appalachian Trail, or, in French, Sentier International des Appalaches.

Like the ancient chain of mountains, the story didn't end when the IAT reached Forillon National Park at the tip of Cap Gaspé in 1999. As the years went by, the trail was extended through the Canadian Maritime Provinces of Newfoundland and Labrador, then Nova Scotia and Prince Edward Island.

In 2009, horizons broadened when a team from the British Geological Survey of Scotland contacted IAT leaders with the hope of linking two existing Scottish trails to the IAT. These geologists were providing technical advice to the new Lochaber Global Geopark, which includes Ben Nevis, the highest mountain in the British Isles. Working together with community and government leaders, the West Highland Way and the Cape Wrath Trail, which passes through the North West Highlands Geopark, were added as the first European sections of the IAT.

This IAT chapter in Scotland was quickly followed by others in Greenland, Norway, Sweden, Denmark, the Netherlands, England, Ireland, and Wales. Since then, Iceland, the Isle of Man, Spain, France, Portugal, and Morocco have also joined. Many of these countries have active trail sections, and others, like Norway, Sweden, Denmark, and France, soon may.

From the start, the IAT has blossomed, promoting and impacting rural economic development and fulfilling the dream of nations working together. In 2011, a group of IAT leaders met at the Gîte de Mont Albert in Québec's Parc de la Gaspésie, to adopt a Structure and Responsibilities document and to welcome France as the newest chapter of the IAT Council.

This memorandum of understanding gives each chapter—which must represent a country, province, or state—an equal voice. Each chapter has autonomy over their route, with priority given to following the ancient Appalachian/Caledonian landscape and connecting directly to the routes of adjacent chapters. The International IAT Council serves as a central forum to discuss ideas, share successes, and address problems. Decisions are made in good faith and sealed with a handshake.

The concepts of unification and thinking beyond borders are no less vital today. To see this collaboration in action, we need look no further than the Ulster–Ireland Chapter of the IAT. Encompassing segments in both Northern Ireland and the Republic of Ireland, this chapter is keenly focused on promoting eco and geotourism in their region. A North American delegation including experts on both the AT and IAT traveled to Strabane, Northern Ireland, in June 2019 to participate in a forum on the potential impacts of the IAT on the outdoor economy.

From the Loop Road, the very first thirty miles of the IAT cross the national monument. Beyond the monument, the trail continues through Maine for more than one hundred miles before reaching New Brunswick. One might wonder why the IAT does not begin atop Katahdin, where the AT ends. In years past, hikers were permitted to descend from Katahdin following the Katahdin Lake Trail to the Katahdin Lake East entrance to Baxter. As recently as 2017, the Baxter State Park visitor publication *Wildnotes* included the IAT, stating, "Another distance trail, the International Appalachian Trail, also features Baxter Peak, this time as the southern terminus of the trail that is still developing." It went on to list the countries the IAT crossed and gave the IAT website address.

This entrance to Baxter State Park is now closed and the trail to it overgrown and almost impassable. After the Loop Road was constructed in 2012, and improved in the years afterward, more and more visitors began informally accessing the park from that direction. This put too much people pressure on the area around Katahdin Lake, which was being managed as a semi-wilderness. Since the closure of this gate, hikers can still connect Baxter Peak to the IAT in several ways, none of which is yet official.

Maine's IAT chapter is currently working with Baxter State Park, the National Park Service, the Nature Conservancy, and other local landowners to establish an authorized route connecting the summit of Katahdin with the monument's Loop Road.

By now, you may not be too surprised to learn that the IAT has the potential to grow in the southern United States as well, making use of two existing trails. A portion of Georgia's Benton MacKaye Trail, not yet officially part of the IAT, runs seventy miles south from Springer Mountain to connect with the Pinhoti National Recreation Trail. The Pinhoti, in turn, follows the Southern Appalachian range for 337 miles to Alabama's Flagg Mountain, the southernmost Appalachian peak over 1,000 feet. Pinhoti hikers follow light blue blazes and diamond-shaped white trail markers, emblazoned with a black turkey track, in honor of the Creek Indian word *pinhoti*, which means "turkey home."

As of 2020, there are approximately five thousand miles of well-maintained trail designated as part of the IAT, although some segments, such as the Ulster Way, also retain their traditional names. With the anticipated addition of significant new sections in Europe, primarily in France, and the possibility of the Georgia–Alabama extension, the total distance along the IAT and AT combined would surpass ten thousand miles. That's quite a walk!

Just like that, I had become a solo backpacker for the first time in a long time. Without the canoe, of course, my load was far lighter than I was used to. Gone were the paddles, the PFD, the cushy canoe chair, the yoke, and even my bathing suit. My gear and supplies were whit-

First night out, Wassataquoik campsite, Katahdin Woods and Waters National Monument

tled down to a backpack weighing twenty-four pounds, including five days of food and one quart of water.

That first night out, the monument embraced me with open arms. There was no one else around, and I had a choice between the large, clean Wassataquoik (Wah-*sat*-a-cook) lean-to or the adjacent camp-site, both with picnic tables and the shared use of the privy. Currently, campsites and lean-to shelters within the monument are available on a first-come first-serve basis, with no fee. Dogs are not permitted in the shelters. Campfires at these sites require a free fire permit from the Maine Forest Service.

I set up my tent beneath tall pines, beside Katahdin Brook, which feeds into nearby Wassataquoik Stream. After a refreshing splash in the cool water, I went exploring. Just beyond the campsite, the trail crossed the brook on a dilapidated old bridge where I met a garter snake stretched out in the sun.

Supper was spicy, hearty chicken gumbo. My backpacking sup-pers would all be healthy dehydrated meals from Good To-Go, a Maine company located in Kittery. I built a campfire. I've learned to enjoy them when I can because you never know what the next eve-ning may bring.

It had taken three hours to hike the five-plus miles, but I hadn't been hurrying. About a third of a mile from the parking area, the trail crossed a bridge over Katahdin Brook just within the monument boundary. Nearby was a sturdy, new-looking lean-to. In the lean-to journal, a note from "Cloudwalker" announced the start of his IAT thru-hike on July 4th, just four days earlier.

Soon, I met a family of four walking out to the only car in the parking area. Now I was truly alone. Ahead, the sandy logging road rose for a long distance, ramrod straight. The first pile of moose poop made for an exciting moment. Abandoned overgrown logging roads also have ever-changing roadside gardens. Today, butterflies flitted among Joe Pye weed, daisies, pearly everlasting, yellow hawkweed, and a small yellow flower that reminded me of butter and eggs.

After climbing a hot and buggy mile, the IAT turned right onto a similar road barricaded by a row of boulders. I was planning a side trip to climb Barnard Mountain, elevation 1,621 feet. Convinced this was the turnoff to climb the mountain, I hid my backpack in the woods and went on, walking light as a feather. I didn't feel so euphoric a while later when I reached the point where the Barnard Mountain trail actually departed from the IAT. Sheepishly, I backtracked to get my stuff and vowed to study the map and trail guide more closely.

I was following the 2018 Maine IAT Trail Guide, accessed from the website of the Maine Chapter of the International Appalachian Trail. It was a simple typed document, listing turns and landmarks, with distances given to the tenth of a mile. Its entries would prove to be accurate and comprehensive. The route was marked with small white rectangular metal signs with light blue letters, reading IAT-SIA.

Another mistake was not admitting that the bugs swarming me were black flies. These are the worst of the pests that assault the Maine hiker and the inspiration for the state's "bug season" in late spring and early summer. The gnat-sized black fly focuses its ferocious attack on the hairline, ears, and areas like the waistline, where it can squeeze in under tight clothing. On me, and many others, the bite, often dripping blood, becomes a hard, itchy welt that lingers for several days.

Yes, I should have dug out my head net and bug spray when I paused for a long drink of water. Ditching my backpack once more, in a raspberry patch, I turned right onto the real trail up the mountain.

It was nice to be on a shaded woods trail, comfortable underfoot, meandering through the young forest of beech, maple, and birch. I hadn't gone far when something rounded and brown, like the back of a box turtle, moved among the ferns and baby maples. It was a ruffed grouse, the bird fondly known to Mainers as the *pa'tridge*.

She turned her crested head to look at me with one dark eye and let her wings drop. Their intricate coloration mimicked the shades and textures of the fallen leaves. Each part of her body had a different pattern, brown feathers broken up by darker bands and brighter chevrons, like sparkles of sun on the forest floor. She was beautiful. Slowly she eased away, keeping a certain safe distance between us. She probably had a nest, or little ones. Zigzagging back and forth across the trail, she enticed me on with brief pauses and soft, feeble calls. When we'd gone far enough, she turned away.

The trail went on, passing through a long, narrow cleft between

Scenes from the climb to the summit of Barnard Mountain

two giant boulders, several times my height, then climbing more steeply through open hemlock and spruce. I read on the map that the switchbacks and solid stone steps had been built in 2014 by the Maine Conservation Corps. Soon, glimpses of blue sky drew me upward, and I knew the summit must be close.

Emerging into the open, a broad granite outcropping with a new picnic table commanded a regal view. A large dark raptor rode the thermals well below me, floating brown against the pillowy folds of verdant green. I was sad that I had decided against the weight of carrying binoculars. To the west, sun glinted white off Katahdin Lake at the threshold of Baxter State Park. On an informational display along the interstate, I'd read that Katahdin Lake had been added to Baxter in 2006. From Katahdin Lake, Katahdin Brook flows through tiny Rocky Pond and into the monument.

Wind washed the summit and me free of cares, until it faded, and the black flies found me.

Bug-propelled, I scrambled down to my backpack and grabbed my head net and spray. One old logging road led to another, this one with a name and a sign. To the right, the Wassataquoik Stream Tote Road would take me a half-mile to the lean-to and campsite. To the left, it was a mile and a half to Orin Falls. I decided against hiking three extra miles roundtrip, but later read that this is one of the most alluring cascades in the monument. That night, listening to the gurgle of the brook from my cozy sleeping bag, I wished I'd gone.

I woke often in the soft warm night, a myriad of stars above and blinking fireflies below.

CHAPTER 7

FINDING MY WAY

Whence these legends and traditions,
With the odors of the forest,
With the dew and damp of meadows,
With the curling smoke of wigwams,
With the rushing of great rivers,
With their frequent repetitions,
And their wild reverberations
As of thunder in the mountains?

—**Henry Wadsworth Longfellow,** *The Song of Hiawatha*

Fording vigorous streams is a rite of passage for Maine's long-distance hikers. Anticipation roused me early the following morning, and I stepped softly on the leaf-strewn road in hopes of spotting a moose. When I came to Wassataquoik Stream standing squarely in my path, I smiled at the sight of the brown sign with the single word FORD. The crossing was perhaps 150 feet wide. In the morning sun, the water babbled brightly over rocks washed clean by the flow, beckoning me onward.

I hung my boots around my neck by their strings and strapped on my Tevas. Using my hiking poles for balance, I slowly crossed, feeling just a gentle pull from the current. The water, at its deepest, was still well below my knees. During the snowmelt of spring, conditions would be very different. The trail guide warned in bold print,

"This stream is prone to flash flooding. Use care and do not camp on any gravel bars during rain events."

At first, I couldn't spot the matching FORD sign on the far bank. I walked upstream a bit, then dumped my stuff and wandered downstream through the edge of the woods. I found one of the familiar IAT/SIA signs on a peeling birch, several hundred feet downstream from where I'd crossed.

For a mile, the path wound along beside the stream. Walking kept me at a slower pace, and when I came to a brilliant Canada lily, I could simply stop to admire it. The angle of the sun was just right for revealing the secrets of the clear rocky stream, and I searched the deeper pools for brook trout. This was a well-traveled trail, reminiscent of the places I loved best in Shenandoah National Park.

I shuffled carefully across a beaver dam, then turned left where the route of the IAT joined the Old Keep Path. For a short while, I would be walking on history, along a popular mid-nineteenth-century route to Katahdin. Though the mountain lies within Baxter State Park, the journeys of many early climbers began here, along the East Branch and Wassataquoik Stream. To understand this part of monument history, we must look beyond its boundaries, to the west, to the peak that Thoreau knew as K'taadn. We must begin with the Penobscot, who viewed its towering heights with awe and reverence.

The story that follows is based on the typewritten notes of writer Fannie Hardy Eckstorm, preserved in the University of Maine archives. Eckstorm's extensive travels and study of Maine folklore and native culture in the early twentieth century are widely recognized. Her notes, for a presentation about Maine Indian legends, begin with a passage from Longfellow's *Song of Hiawatha*. Her summary was composed after listening to an older Penobscot friend recite the Katahdin legend four times, in two languages. "This is the blending of the versions," Eckstorm wrote, "the most of it in her very words." I hope I do justice to the spirit of that Penobscot elder in my telling of the tale.

Long ago, in the silken smoothness of a summer night, a host of stars filled the ebony sky. The silhouettes of spruce and fir were faintly visible, encircling the camp. The flicker of firelight danced on the lined face of the storyteller, in whose eyes and voice lived the history of his people.

The lands on which we walk were young, he began, drawing in even those who had heard the tale for a lifetime, *and the spirit of K'taadn watched over the people, even as he does today.*

One bright morning, in the time of berries, a young woman wandered on the shoulders of the mountain. Higher and higher she went, filling her birchbark basket. Her busy hands worked, but her mind began to dream of other things. Above her rose the rugged rocky slopes, until they seemed to disappear into sky and clouds.

"Oh, how strong K'taadn is," she thought, and then she began to dance and sing among the rocks. "K'taadn, K'taadn," she sang to the mountain, "you are as fierce as a warrior in the heat of battle. What a man you would be. Nothing could hurt you, nothing could touch you. Not the bite of winter cold or the fury of the blackest storm. Always you would stand strong. But even if you were a man, I would never marry you. Never, no, never, I would grow old before I married you."

Now the young woman possessed great beauty, but she was very bold to sing and dance this way, at the feet of mighty K'taadn. Her beauty was as the first hint of pink in the dawn sky. Delicate as the spotted fawn, shining as the lily, sweet as the sugar that the maple gives us.

Listen, though, when I say that she was very bold to sing and dance this way. As her words blew away with the wind, a strange dreamy weariness came over her and she stretched out in the warm sun. Surprisingly, her sleep was peaceful. How long she slept I do not know, but when her eyes gently opened, there before her stood a man. Tall and proud as the cedar, his shoulders strong, his chest broad, with muscles rippled and gnarled as the flanks of the mountain on which he stood.

My children, did you guess that the man who gazed down upon her beauty was K'taadn?

The man took the woman for his wife, and they made their home deep inside the mountain. Theirs was a fine wigwam, with all the moose meat and blueberries she could eat. In time, the woman gave K'taadn a son, strong and healthy, but with eyebrows just like stone. They named him

Katahdinosis. Many moons passed, and a longing grew within the woman to visit her people. This K'taadn granted.

"Go, see your people," he instructed, "take our son, but do not allow anyone to make a bow and arrows for him." These seemed strange words, but the young mother remembered them.

As the boy grew, he discovered that a special power had been granted to him. By bending his left finger like a little bow and laying his right over it like an arrow, he could kill birds and moose just by pointing. This gift greatly helped his people in their times of hunger.

What need did the small boy have for a real bow and arrows?

In the spring, when the salmon ran, the boy's mother went to the river with some of her family, leaving the little boy with his grandfather. The old man was pleased. As the days passed, he worked by his fire, shaping a fine piece of ash into a small bow. No one can say if the mother of Katahdinosis had ever told him not to.

At last the bow and arrows were finished, and he took the eager boy into the forest to practice. To his grandfather's delight, Katahdinosis listened with respect and learned so quickly that it seemed some magic spirit must be in him. Over and over, the small arrows struck the old stump at which he aimed. All went well, until the sun began to drop low in the sky.

One arrow had been lost among the thick bushes. As the grandfather searched, the boy drew back the bow for one last shot. Thinking his grandfather was behind him, he let the arrow fly.

Word of the accident soon reached the river, and the people hurried home, their canoes filled with fish and their hearts with sorrow. But by then, it was too late. The grandfather lay dead, and K'taadn had returned to bring his family home.

That small family must have grown, the storyteller ended, as the children listened wide-eyed.

For when the mountain roars and howls in the storm, and we think it is the wind, their voices speak. Listen closely and you will hear the music of their flutes. Look closely on a winter night and you may glimpse the light of their fire. For they dwell within the mountain still.

Majestic Katahdin drew the attention of explorers and settlers just as surely as the Penobscot and filled the dreams of many who gazed upon it. The first recorded European sighting dates to 1783, when surveyor Joseph Chadwick and his party were returning from Québec along the West Branch. After viewing the mountain, they heard from the Penobscot that it was the highest in the land.

"They can ascend so high as Greens Grow & no higher," Chadwick wrote, referring to the traditional spiritual belief of the Penobscot, who never went above the timberline on Katahdin. Interestingly, signs often warn modern-day hikers to be cautious when ascending above the timberline, where weather conditions are more extreme and can swiftly change. Perhaps this ancient precept wisely guarded the physical well-being of the people as well.

Interestingly, two Penobscot men served as guides during the first recorded ascent of Katahdin. In August 1804, surveyor Charles Turner, Jr. and his companions reached the summit, where they left a lead sheet with their initials and the date, under a bottle of rum. That ascent, and the two that followed in 1819 and 1820, originated from the south along the West Branch. Historians believe the routes of the climbers roughly followed the present-day Hunt and Abol trails.

Maine achieved statehood on March 15, 1820, separating from the state of Massachusetts. The Maine Boundary Commission was soon formed, its responsibility to survey the new state and lay out townships. In fact, the third recorded ascent of Katahdin, in 1820, was part of that endeavor. John W. Neff, author of *Katahdin: An Historic Journey*, notes one of the major accomplishments of that expedition.

"This expedition provided the most accurate measurement of the mountain's height at the time. While Turner had estimated Katahdin's height to be nearly 13,000 feet, the 1820 expedition set its height to be 5,385 feet. This estimation, formulated using only a British barometer, was a mere 118 feet more than the actual height—not bad for the instruments being used at the time."

Long before and well to the east, on the border with the Canadian province of New Brunswick, surveyors had banded a yellow birch tree with an iron hoop, to serve as a permanent marker. From that precise spot, which marked the source of the St. Croix River on Monument Brook, the international boundary was run straight north. That tree would soon be the starting point for another survey that would bring the first two people up Katahdin from the east, rather than the south. The Maine Boundary Commission had decided to lay out the new townships in a grid, based on a line that would be run due west from that historic spot.

That line came to be called the Monument Line.

So, if you're looking at a map of Katahdin Woods and Waters and notice a line cutting through the middle, it is not a monument boundary, as I first thought. It's just a line with lots of history, that happens to be called the Monument Line. From that line, six-mile-square townships were laid out in a grid across northern Maine. DeLorme's *The Maine Atlas and Gazetteer*, the quintessential resource for exploring the state, reveals many townships that still carry their original designations. I would soon be entering T3 R7 WELS, which stands for Township 3, Range 7, West of the Easterly Line of the State. Township numbers increase from south to north and range numbers increase from east to west.

In 1825, surveyor Joseph C. Norris, Sr. and his son headed west from that old yellow birch, nearing the East Branch by late September. Other work called them away for over a month, and it was early November before they could return. On November 11, extremely late in the season for an attempt on Katahdin, the pair struggled to reach the summit. They had crossed the East Branch and the wild Wassataquoik Valley, through what is now the national monument, in the first recorded ascent from the east. In a remarkable feat, they cut a line, straight and true, through very rugged terrain, finishing atop Katahdin over a month later than Baxter State Park currently recommends climbing. Two decades would pass before anyone else approached the mountain from that direction.

Katahdin is a complex mountain with multiple peaks, the highest being Baxter Peak. Approaching from the east, climbers would first top Pamola Peak, then cross the Knife Edge to Baxter. The Knife Edge is just that—a narrow ridge, in places only a couple of feet wide, that falls away abruptly on either side.

Pamola Peak is named for another fearsome character of Indian legend, the one most responsible for keeping the Penobscot away from the summit. I chose to have my storyteller focus on the man-spirit of the mountain, but the legends of Pamola, the Penobscots' Thunder God, are more numerous.

For one person's interpretation of these tales, we can turn to *Chimney Pond Tales: Yarns Told by Leroy Dudley*, preserved and assembled by Clayton Hall. Roy Dudley guided at Chimney Pond, in one of Katahdin's high mountain basins, from the 1890s until his death in 1942. He was respected both for his intimate knowledge of the area and his tall tales around the campfire.

I will let Roy describe Pamola, as he first saw him.

"He stood up about eighteen or twenty feet tall, with body and legs like a man, but all covered with coarse hair like a moose. His head was like a moose and his ears and horns, but he had kind of a big curved beak like an eagle. He had a great long beard on his chin (and his feet) had three great pointed toes like a chicken, and one that pointed backwards. He had big wings growing out of his shoulders, but just like a bat's wings. He was a fierce looking sight!"

In the 1930s, Clayton Hall carried an old-fashioned wax cylinder dictating machine the seven miles to Chimney Pond, found Roy, and recorded and transcribed his stories. Many years later, Hall's manuscript was discovered by his niece, Elizabeth Hall Harmon. Together with artist and illustrator Jane Thomas, who had known Roy and his stories, Harmon published *Chimney Pond Tales*. This priceless piece of Maine folklore expertly weaves the tricky and sometimes malevolent Pamola into the antics of a lifetime dedicated to guiding.

By the 1830s, two families had carved out farms along the East Branch that could be reached by road from Stacyville. The Hunt and Dacey farms were both located within the national monument, and I planned to explore one or both sites while canoeing the river in a few weeks. Both became important stopping points for travelers, the last vestiges of civilization before entering the wilds.

The Reverend Marcus R. Keep was a home missionary in Fort Kent when he first explored the lower slopes of Katahdin in 1846. By the following summer, he had triumphantly led a party of fellow ministers to the summit from the east, first stopping at Hunt Farm. A unique and eccentric individual, Keep was almost too full of energy and self-confidence. Undoubtedly a natural leader, he had a vision of the importance of the mountain and would lead many parties up the mountain in the years to come.

Access from the east improved as lumbering operations commenced in earnest. By 1848, a tote road for hauling logs stretched along the north side of Wassataquoik Stream, from the East Branch to Katahdin Lake. From the lake, it was only another five miles to the foot of Avalanche Slide, the rockslide by which Keep had reached Pamola Peak in 1847. In June 1848, Keep and young woodsman John Stacy finished the trail that would come to be known as the Keep Path. It was the first trail to Katahdin. For many years, Keep climbed Katahdin annually, guiding a host of friends, as well as geologists, botanists, and other scientists to the summit.

By the mid-1870s, parts of the Keep Path were overgrown and obscured by continued logging operations, and other roads and trails became more popular.

In 1860, the Maine state legislature granted to Marcus Keep the title to two hundred acres of land at the outlet of Katahdin Lake, where he had built a camp in a small clearing. Today, Keep Ridge, on Baxter State Park's Helon Taylor Trail, honors the explorer's contribution to Katahdin history.

So, I followed the Old Keep Path for a short while, as if I were returning to Stacyville from a triumphant ascent with the feisty reverend as my guide. Soon, though, the IAT turned left once more, heading toward Deasey Mountain, the monument's highest peak.

Earl's Erratic dwarfed me. Rising in lichen-crusted grandeur high above my head, this house-sized boulder stood as a testament to the mighty power of glacial action. Discovered by Maine IAT board member and trail-builder Earl Raymond, this granddaddy of all rocks was plunked down in the middle of a stand of mature hardwood, right beside the trail. It seemed a hard-to-miss landmark. However, Raymond later explained to me that the trail had been carefully routed to pass by his namesake rock.

The immense chunk of Ordovician basalt had most likely been

carried from the cliffs of Deasey Mountain, just a few miles away. It was deposited by the glacier in an area of similar bedrock and, consequently, was not a true glacial erratic, which must differ in rock type from the underlying bedrock.

The trail gradually ascended the shoulder of Deasey Mountain. Far below, I caught glimpses of the East Branch, though I never found the short side trail to a viewpoint mentioned in the trail guide. Official IAT markers were scarcer now, and I was often following bits of blue, or sometimes orange, flagging. Often it was just the smallest piece, stretched tight, as if the trail builder had only the end of a roll to work with. Sawed off logs were another hint of the way to go. In places, intuition was the only clue to which thin opening might be the path.

I did what I've done before. Gave up and sat down to eat my lunch, while hoping the short rest would clear my mind. Sure enough, after the break, there was the trail, right where it was supposed to be.

Now I walked in the hushed air of a forest cathedral. Ancient hemlocks roofed the open forest, creating vistas deep into the woods, which rose high on the left and dropped away on my right. A bear should be ambling here, I thought, in this place so like the Shenandoah trail where my son Taylor and I had spotted our first black bear when he was only seven. I climbed the east ridge of Deasey, then descended, elevation that unfortunately would have to be regained.

The trail brought me to a sparkling clear stream. This was the last reliable water source before tonight's campsite, still three-plus miles and two mountaintops away. I filtered just one bottle of water, gambling that it would be enough to keep me hydrated without adding too much weight.

I should have drunk and filtered more.

Beside the stream was an old cabin, painted a faded barn red with white trim. The roof on the two back rooms, probably the kitchen and bedroom, had long since collapsed. I explored the front room, a porch encircled by generous windows. Rough handmade cabinets and tables, built into the walls, held chipped enamelware pots, old bottles, and a hefty, rusted iron kettle. Here, the fire wardens of Deasey Mountain had made their home. Season after hard-working season, in all weather, theirs was a simple life lived out in an atmosphere of great solitude and beauty, with a window on the woods.

Exploring the abandoned fire warden cabin on Deasey Mountain

I felt a peace in this spot and sensed the mute memories of a long-gone way of life.

Later, I was given a glimpse into several summers spent here in the late 1940s. On July 5, 1947, Ed Werler, his wife, Mary Jane, and their two dogs arrived here for the first time, after a long canoe trip and a two-mile uphill climb. They did not even know in advance how many rooms the cabin had. MJ carried a radio, her ukulele, and a loaded backpack. Ed carried an Army duffle, lineman's tools, and extra insulators to repair the telephone wire strung along the route. Sometimes, the lines came down when a moose became entangled in the wire. The couple would have a crank phone connecting the cabin and tower with each other and the Maine Forest Service in Stacyville.

In his book, *The Call of Katahdin*, Ed tells of life as a fire tower lookout. The cabin sat in the middle of a small open clearing, by this same stream, of course. A cave of sorts had been dug into its bank, with wooden walls, roof, and door, to serve as a cold cellar. Inside the cabin, the wood cookstove held a greasy frying pan and the sink dirty dishes. But for a young, ambitious couple who aspired to one day own a Maine sporting camp, it was heaven.

Up on Daicey Mountain, as it was spelled back then, Ed vigilantly kept watch, every day it didn't rain. There were other tasks as well—maintaining the trail, monitoring a rain gauge, cutting stove wood, and conducting an annual insect survey. For fun, Ed and MJ fished, had picnics, and even entertained the more adventurous of their friends. Homemade donuts, with mashed potatoes in the recipe, were "standard procedure in the north country." MJ went through flour in twenty-five-pound bags, baking bread, pies, and cakes as well.

My favorite story comes from their second summer on the mountain, in 1948. Friends of a friend would be flying over and wondered if there was anything they could drop off.

That hot July day, Ed and MJ asked for ice cream!

"Sure enough, when the day came," Ed writes, "MJ and I were at the tower waiting for the delivery. On the first run their plane buzzed the mountain and they waved and yelled 'hellos.' The next run was a little higher, and down floated two little homemade parachutes with containers of vanilla ice cream packed in ice. We had to search some to find them in the bushes, but, oh, didn't that taste good."

While filtering water at the stream, I'd been startled to see a man appear along the trail, from the direction in which I'd come. He looked to be my age or a bit older and carried a professional camera and tripod that either lent authenticity or were the perfect cover for a serial murderer. *Where do thoughts like these come from?* I wondered.

After a brief hello and mutual guessing at how far it was to the summit, he continued up the trail.

I didn't know how I felt about company, but Glenn turned out to be all right. Together we slogged our way up the steep slope, a nine-hundred-foot elevation gain in under a mile.

Emerging onto the rocky ledges near the top, I caught my first glimpse of a white building framed by twisted, wind-worn spruce. This was Ed's unusual fire lookout, referred to alternately as a ground cab or fire cab. A fire tower minus the tower. Anchored to the rock by four strong guy wires, it had stood strong since 1929. On this pinnacle of granite, among the blueberry bushes and moose poop, fire wardens had scanned this priceless 360-degree view for any hint of smoke.

Inside the weathered white building stood an excellent example of an original Osborne Firefinder, used by the fire lookout to pinpoint the location of wildfires. After leveling the instrument each morning, the warden would tighten the horsehair sight. If he were short of real horsehair, black thread or thin wire could be used instead. Sighted in properly, the instrument and its accompanying map would give the angle, elevation, and approximate distance to the telltale smoke. When the smoke was visible from two or more towers, the location of the fire could be quite accurately plotted by triangulation. The map, I noticed, was titled "LOOKOUT MAP—DAICEY MT."

Glenn, not surprisingly, turned out to be a photographer and writer. He had visited the monument twice before. He'd also climbed, it seemed, every one of the numerous surrounding mountains and could name them all. Best of all, he kindly shared a disposable lens wipe for my smeared and sweaty glasses, so I could fully appreciate the incredible view.

Glenn left first, having to hike all the way back to his car.

The Deasey Mountain fire cab contains an original Osborne Firefinder

Since starting out, I had been consulting the detailed Loop Road map, with its helpful topo lines. Unfortunately, I was about to walk off its edge. I turned off on the trail toward adjacent Lunksoos Mountain. After descending for a while, I began to doubt myself, as the trail so closely resembled the way I'd climbed up from the fire warden cabin. I turned back toward the summit, found a sign, and oriented myself, discovering that I'd been on the correct trail after all. After dropping down three hundred feet through another majestic hemlock forest, the trail began to climb once more.

On the open ledges near the top of Lunksoos, I came to a spot where the rock cairns I'd been following simply gave out. There were none ahead that I could see. My GPS map showed a little triangle marking the peak, so I navigated toward that instead. After one dead end, where a cliff dropped sharply away into thin air, I found my way to an ancient dilapidated wooden sign that read, INTERNATIONAL AT, LUNKSOOS MTN, ELEV 1811 FT. I didn't recall having seen signs marking the other summits.

Far below shone the blue waters of the East Branch, the only break in a sea of forest. The faraway mountains were blurred a hazy blue, even on this clear and sunny afternoon.

By now, I was taking nothing for granted. On the way up, I'd placed little spruce tips or maple leaves on the cairns, so I could discern the upward trail. Truly, all the trails looked so much alike. The descent across lichen-covered ledges went fine, but before long I was confused again and beginning to wish that I'd filled both bottles of water.

I'd left the cairns behind and dropped back into the woods, when I lost the trail for good. Far fewer hikers came this way and finding signs or bits of flagging was essential. At one point, the trail just seemed to vanish. Over and over, I doubled back to the same trail marker not far from an orange-flagged tree. Beyond that, I could find nothing. I needed to go west, where the sun hung lower in the sky with each passing minute of frustration.

Thinking of survival training, I did many things right. Finding a shady spot, I sat down, drank the last of my water, and pulled out all my resources. With me, I had a page from an old DeLorme Atlas, with good topo lines, but no IAT route; a small computer printout of the IAT map with the topo lines unreadable; and the map page on my GPS. Thankfully, those following in my footsteps would soon have access to the new Katahdin Woods and Waters waterproof trail map.

I was lost, or at least at a loss as to where to go next. The distance to the Lunksoos lean-to was probably no more than a mile, but this was thick forest, and I had no water left. Dusk would come soon, and I would be forced to camp, no matter where I found myself.

CHAPTER 8

LIVELY WATERS

Deep calls to deep in the roar of your waterfalls.

—Psalm 42:7

I sat for a long time, pondering the maps, the bugs and heat forgotten, until I was sure.

It was enough. My target was an old tote road, which would surely be recognizable if I reached it. To get there, I would walk west and downhill, to a gully with a small brook that I had found on the DeLorme Atlas page. I could fill up on water, then follow the contour line at the edge of the gully to the road. If all went according to plan.

The brook appeared even sooner than the map indicated. Quickly, I filtered a bottle of water and drank my fill. I now knew for sure where I was. Continuing west, the open hardwood forest gradually transitioned to dense young spruce, but I stayed true to my line, watching my progress on the GPS map. I was a martyr to the bugs and the thick underbrush, but I hardly noticed.

Eventually, shades of lighter green peeked through ahead, and I prayed that it was the old road. Fighting through the last of the thick stuff, I popped out into the open. I was covered with welts and scratches oozing blood, but that didn't matter. This was obviously an old road, grown up now in tall, deep green ferns. And there, nailed to a tree, was the familiar white and blue rectangle of an IAT/SIA sign.

The road led to an old log yard, an open clearing where harvested logs were once stacked and loaded. Its utilitarian ugliness looked beautiful to me. The Lunksoos Mountain campsite contained a bright, clean lean-to, picnic table, and plenty of space to set up my tent. The walk to fetch water from a nearby brook was a good three-tenths of a mile roundtrip, with a steep climb down and back up.

Weary and aching, I cooked chili but couldn't eat much. I was probably dehydrated. My nauseous stomach agreed to some tea, and then I headed for bed. When I closed my eyes, I saw the buzzing bombardment of imaginary insects. Neither that, nor the rocky gravel poking through my sleeping pad could keep me awake, though, and I slept deeply for a solid eight hours.

The next morning, I read through the recent entries in the lean-to journal. Cloudwalker, the seventy-two-year-old IAT thru-hiker from Florida, had written this familiar-sounding note:

"There must be some water down there somewhere, but I'm not getting lost in those woods. How far? Need some blazes or blue tape. Second day on IAT—yesterday was a killer—had to camp in the woods when I lost the trail in the dusk. Just a mile from here. An N or S on the blue arrow would help greatly at times. Especially on Lunksoos summit where entrance and exit look identical!"

The stories of calm and uneventful hours are much more quickly told. Scattered thunderstorms in the forecast pushed me quickly along abandoned logging roads and across several small brooks and streams, with brief views of a far-off hazy mountain. Grassy old roads look much the same, but another ruffed grouse flirted with me, and a host of wildflowers in pinks, yellows, purples, and whites brightened the way. I discovered a bleached deer skull and animal droppings and many, many toads. Whenever I started to feel bored, I reminded myself that at least the route was clearly marked and level.

Around five miles from camp, I turned left to go north on the Old Telos Tote Road, which follows the west shore of the river. Shortly, the trail crossed Little Spring Brook, which was marked with a wooden sign. Near this spot, a vital Atlantic salmon fish hatchery had operated from 1903 to 1916.

This facility was not the state's first hatchery. Maine was a pioneer in early conservation efforts, forming a fish commission four years earlier than the federal government. Concern for the Atlantic salmon was evident from the start. The commission's first annual report, dated January 1868, focused strongly on the restoration of the Atlantic salmon. Recommended remedies included the building of fishways over impassable dams, prevention of excessive fishing, breeding of fish in the rivers to be restocked, and "that the waters be not poisoned."

One of the original commissioners, Charles G. Atkins, was a visionary in managing and conserving fisheries, devoting his entire forty-eight-year career to this mission. Did you know that there is a Hall of Fame for fish culturists? In 1996, Atkins was posthumously inducted into the D.C. Booth Historic National Fish Hatchery Fish Culture Hall of Fame in Spearfish, South Dakota, in honor of his life's work.

In 1871, Spencer Baird, head of the newly created federal commission, chose Atkins to locate a site for Maine's first hatchery. Still in operation today, the Craig Brook National Fish Hatchery in Orland raises seven river-specific Atlantic salmon stocks, including one for the Penobscot River.

Later, Atkins traveled to Germany to study fish culturing, as no such training existed in the United States. "His meticulous style in scientific methodology, his accurate data recording and retrieval techniques, the production of his own skillful illustrations dealing with external morphology and embryological development of fish species," all set him apart, explains E. Peter Steenstra, of the US Fish and Wildlife Service. "With his 'Kodak,' Atkins recorded and left us a visual window upon his world—not a vignette, but a *Saturday Evening Post* portrayal of his life's work. He produced hundreds of photographs which illustrate well the process and product of fish culturing in its infancy."

Up in the East Branch, salmon stocking began at the turn of the century. From 1900 to 1903, baby salmon, or "fry," were shipped from Craig Brook for this endeavor. The marathon two-day journey, mostly by train, was dependent on the availability of rail cars. Atkins argued for a simpler, safer, and less expensive solution. It was critically important that the fry arrive at the river in a timely fashion, at the optimum stage in their life cycle. In the spring of 1904, there would be nearly three million fry to ship!

"We are now face to face with a crisis in the propagation of Atlantic salmon," Atkins wrote to the US Commissioner of Fisheries in September 1903. "There is imminent risk of complete failure. I therefore plead again for permission to try the new scheme, of hatching the eggs where the fry can be liberated at the right time in the waters which are their natural home."

Atkins's farsighted proposal, to establish an auxiliary hatchery along Little Spring Brook, was approved. Work commenced on the site that autumn. With great satisfaction, Atkins reported in April 1904, "At Little Spring Brook...we have now in course of incubation about 2,700,000 eggs of migrating salmon, and hope to hatch nearly as many fish, which we propose to liberate as soon as they have attained the proper size. This will be a better blow, by far, than we have struck for many a year in the effort to preserve the salmon of the Penobscot."

The key to success was transporting eggs, rather than fry, from Craig Brook.

In June, commercial fishermen on the main stem of the Penobscot caught adult salmon in weirs and sold them to Craig Brook. In November, the eggs were stripped and fertilized. By early winter, the eggs had developed visible eyes and could be safely shipped. The eyed eggs traveled to Little Spring Brook in metal milk cans, by train, then sled or buckboard wagon.

By April, the eggs had hatched into alevin or sac-fry. At first, the large orange yolk sacs attached to their abdomens dwarfed the tiny salmon. As weeks passed, the yolk sacs were gradually absorbed, providing food for the growing fish and eliminating the need for hatchery staff to feed them. By May or June, the yolk sacs had been fully absorbed, and the fry could feed on their own.

In buckets, covered by blankets or towels to keep them cool, they were ferried by canoe and released at favorable locations along the East Branch. In 1913, the year of maximum production, Little Spring Brook released 3,482,464 Atlantic salmon fry into the East Branch of the Penobscot.

*This 1904 shot by Charles Atkins is the only known
photograph of the Little Spring Brook fish hatchery
(Credit: Lawrence Stolte, The Forgotten Salmon of the Merrimack)*

Records reviewed to date have not revealed conclusively why the Little Spring Brook Hatchery was closed in October 1916. Historic correspondence indicates that budget cuts and the difficulties of accessing the remote location may have been factors. Perhaps the historically large salmon runs of 1915 and 1916 also impacted the decision.

The salmon eggs were placed in wooden troughs inside the hatchery, supplied by water diverted from the brook. Traces of the gravel filtering system and basins are still evident in the streambed above the site. Remains of the well and ovens can also be found in the woods, a mute testimony to those who carefully tended millions of Atlantic salmon eggs through many long harsh winters in this isolated spot.

As I hiked on, there were occasional glimpses of the river, down through the trees on my right. For another three miles, the road alternated between high open woods and low boggy sections, where perfectly formed moose prints crisscrossed the deep mud. At times it was the best of trails, at times the worst. There was no resting, thanks to the bugs, and I finally surrendered and changed into suffocating long pants. The thought of a brisk river cascading over a waterfall began to fill my mind—the dancing waters, misty spray, and my feet immersed in a pool as I simply sat. It sounded divine.

From Grand Lake Matagamon, the East Branch runs southeast for 47.5 miles, descending over four hundred feet to its meeting with the West Branch in the town of Medway. Roughly half of that distance lies within Katahdin Woods and Waters National Monument. The river reaches the monument about a mile below the lake and runs along, or occasionally within, its eastern boundary for over twenty miles. Hunting, except for bear hunting with bait or dogs, is allowed on those monument lands that extend east of the East Branch. This area includes the noncontiguous Seboeis and Hunt Farm parcels. I would see only the latter, from the canoe, as it borders the East Branch.

In its first ten miles, the river drops over two hundred feet, creating a series of impressive falls or pitches. Four of them have mandatory portages. In order from north to south, these are Haskell Rock Pitch, Pond Pitch, Grand Pitch, and The Hulling Machine. There are no trails to The Hulling Machine, which lies on a river bend two-tenths of a mile east of the IAT. Hiking north, the trail provides spectacular views of the other three. Tonight, I would camp at Grand Pitch, the highest of the falls.

It would turn out to be a race with the rain. I hurried through one quick shower, digging out the dollar store disposable poncho that I'd brought in place of a heavier rain jacket. The thin plastic clung to my sweaty body but kept the backpack somewhat dry.

In a small opening, a red sign pointed the way down a short side trail to the historic Bowlin Camps, dating to 1895. At last, there was the river, wide and placid, giving no hint of the turmoil above. I crossed on a narrow suspension footbridge, just ten boards wide, with a reassuringly solid handrail. A short walk led to a large grassy clearing, where inviting log cabins with green roofs mingled with outbuildings. Their design was echoed in the large lodge, which I found locked. I'd been hoping for a cold drink with some new friends, but everyone must have been out having fun. This sporting camp offers many outdoor activities and services, including guided hunting and fishing, canoe shuttles, snowmobiling, and good old family vacations.

A couple of miles beyond Bowlin Camps, the gathering darkness warned of a more intense storm approaching. Rumbles of thunder urged me to walk faster, and soon I could hear the distinctive voice of a major falls. I made it to the spiffy lean-to just in time to gather some dry kindling before the rain began.

Once again, I was the only camper. The storm moved through quickly, and I set up my tent on soft ground at the edge of the woods. My unrolled sleeping bag looked so inviting that I lay down for a half hour. From my window, I gazed out at the forest floor, content to watch for a chipmunk while a maple branch gently brushed the netting and I relaxed, away from the bugs.

The rumbling bass of Grand Pitch soon pulled me down the portage trail to the falls, which stretched the width of the river. Hurtling forward, a churning cascade of unstoppable white dropped twenty feet over jagged ledges into the gorge below. On both sides, the forest clung bravely to the brink of high banks, with a bird's-eye view of the chaos below.

Upriver, peace reigned. When evening came, I sat on a finger of fractured sedimentary rock that jutted out toward some mild whitewater like a pier. Sunset colors tinged the clouds and settled on the water, and I thought of the others who had surely rested here in the flow of years stretching back into the misty past. I heard the rustle of wings, soft and papery, as something flew unseen behind me. To have this place for my own in the soft summer night was a gift. I had found the river, and it was good.

The storm had brought a change in the weather. The air smelled fresh, and a cleansing breeze bent the tops of the fir in front of puffy, pink clouds. This was the first morning that I had the energy to cook oatmeal, warm and loaded with pecans and cranberries. I strolled through the damp forest to photograph a flower I'd seen—a common wood sorrel growing on an ancient mossy log. Above clover-like leaves, the delicate white five-petaled flower was traced with magenta veins and had a dotted yellow center. A white-throated sparrow added his voice to the joy of the morning.

This would be my last day on the trail before reaching a commercial campground just beyond the monument boundary. Hiking northwest, I would scout the two remaining mandatory portages, then Stair Falls, which I was contemplating running in the canoe. The IAT wound along a high narrow ridge, which I guessed to be an esker. These distinctive deposits of sand and gravel had formed as meltwater flowed through long tunnels beneath thick glacial ice. There were occasional sparkling glimpses of the river, and the sun found its way down through the canopy, illuminating the emerald greens of fern and leaf.

It was less than a half-mile to the next falls, Pond Pitch. Both Grand Pitch and Pond Pitch have portage trails and campsites on both sides of the river, giving paddlers a rare choice of accommodations. One look, though, and I knew that I wanted to camp right here, at Pond Pitch West, on my way down the river. The attractive nook in the young hardwood forest perched beside the river, where it sprang nimbly down ten feet of rocky ledges. There was a picnic table and fire ring, but no privy. The portage trail measured a short 0.15 miles. Picturing what the takeout would look like from the canoe, my landmark would be a cove with a downed birch tree and small rock offshore, just past an island.

I took a detour that morning. Across the IAT from the river, a brown wooden sign pointed the way toward Little Messer Pond, giving its distance as a surprisingly exact .46 miles. Curious and filled with morning-fresh energy, I decided to explore. The blue blazes at the beginning transitioned to occasional orange flagging, then the now-familiar absence of any hint of where the trail continued. Luckily, I had my GPS map, on which the pond was clearly visible. After passing the sister of Earl's Erratic, I followed a snowmobile trail, then struck off through woods until I could see blue water through the trees.

Morning peace on Little Messer Pond

What a discovery! In the stillness of morning, the mirrored surface was broken only by the dimples of rising fish. Across the pond, mountains backed an even row of pointed spires, in a wavy ridge that was repeated in perfect detail on the water. Dragonflies cruised on patrol, their reflections visible among those of the pickerel weed for the briefest of moments. Golden light touched the far treetops. My breathing hushed, I watched the sun bathe the far shore, and it was as if it were bathing my soul, in an hour that I would long remember. *This is why I came.*

CHAPTER 9

MEETING GOOSE AND MAVERICK

Faith is the substance of things hoped for, the evidence of things not seen.

—Hebrews 11:1

Reluctantly, I rose and slowly stretched, knowing that there were still many miles ahead. Backtracking along the snowmobile trail, I found the spruce branch I'd left to mark the turn off toward the river. At the crest of a steep hill, I could faintly hear falling water. Taking a shortcut, I plunged straight down the steep slope, toward the sound. I almost ran, recklessly grabbing tree after tree like a kid, to keep from falling. It was a fun descent.

The IAT never did meander along the river shore as I had pictured it would. However, the lovely wooded road it followed was wide and smooth. About a half-mile from Pond Pitch, Little Messer Pond Road turned off to the left. A sign pointed the way to the Big Spring Brook Hut, three miles away, available by reservation only. The monument's only other cabin, Haskell Hut, lay about a mile north on the IAT. It was open for day use only from May to October but could be reserved overnight in the winter. Currently, there is no fee for the use of these cabins, but dogs are not allowed.

Haskell Rock Pitch is unquestionably the most unique rapid in the monument. About a mile upriver from Pond Pitch, a path led from the IAT to a viewpoint along the portage trail. The rapid takes its name from massive Haskell Rock, a strangely sculpted midriver formation that towers high above the water about halfway through the long stretch of whitewater. Sadly, the rock, in turn, is named for a river driver who died there long ago.

The character of the rock in this area differs greatly from that of the monument's many glacial erratics and mountaintop ledges. Instead of igneous crystallized granite or basalt, this is sedimentary conglomerate, a mishmash of seemingly whatever had been on hand. Examining the rock more closely, I saw rounded stones up to the size of softballs and smaller rougher irregular rocks in shades from orange to gray, all glued together by what had once been sand or mud. The result barely looked substantial enough to have withstood the test of time. In fact, erosion had been hard at work, effectively sculpting the rock into the many fanciful shapes that stood before me.

"Conglomerate forms in places of rapid erosion and deposition… near shorelines or in fast-moving streams, where stones of various sizes are deposited together," explained the Thoreau–Wabanaki Trail map. "The Haskell Rock conglomerate…contains stones of volcanic rock, slate, sandstone, black chert, quartz diorite, and milky quartz.

The fantastically eroded shape of Haskell Rock towers above the river

Erosion has begun to eat into the sides of the rock and will continue to wear away the pedestal until eventually the rock topples into the river."

Another valuable resource for the East Branch (and Webster Brook) is a DeLorme booklet entitled *Maine Geographic Canoeing Volume 3: Northern Rivers,* written by Zip Kellogg and now out of print.

Kellogg mentions the presence of fossils in this coarse conglomerate. I wished I had more time to search for some. Instead, I discovered a small purple bell-shaped flower swaying in the wind, clinging to slender crevices among the gnarled rock. The flowers, some uplifted, some nodding, grew on stems with long, thin leaves. At the base of the stems were clusters of much rounder, slightly notched leaves of an entirely different shape. In this delicate flower, called the harebell or bluebell (*Campanula rotundifolia*), dwelt the hardy tenacity essential for survival along this wild, beautiful river.

Haskell Rock Pitch must be portaged on the west bank. Walking upriver to investigate the takeout, I spotted something green in the river. Not the green of nature, but of man. Working my way down to the shore for a clearer view, I saw it was the crumpled remains of a green canoe, undulating endlessly up and down in a chute of whitewater. Who could say how long it had been there or what tale of disaster had delivered the boat into the river's grasp?

The portage began at the Haskell Deadwater Campsite, which looked as if it had once been a hunting camp. Inside a utilitarian metal shed, a shelf held a pair of discarded hiking boots, salt and pepper shakers, and a stick of deodorant. Outside, a heavy rusted iron chain dangled from a tree where antlered bucks had once hung. Perhaps this had been one of the leased camps from the days when this land was owned by Great Northern Paper. I did not find the site particularly appealing, but a roof over your head and a nice privy would no doubt look heavenly on a rainy day.

The start of the portage would be easy to find as I came down the river. It was well marked, with both a brown wooden sign and an eye-catching yellow one. Just upstream was the mile-long Haskell Deadwater, a slow-moving wide section of river. After paddling the deadwater, I would look on river right for a small marshy cove with a gravel beach and the two distinctive signs.

Returning to the IAT, the road passed through an open area that had probably once been a beaver pond. Boggy pools of dark oily water gleamed among tall grasses beneath a gray-brown stand of dead spruce. The tree skeletons, some leaning at crazy angles, looked forlorn. Although the overall effect was somber, there was beauty here, too, and a habitat that was critically important to wildlife. I smiled to see spiky yellow clumps of swamp candle, a wildflower that I'd come to know along the sandy river bends of the NFCT. The blue-green foliage of tamarack, Maine's only deciduous conifer, was also common here.

The turnoff to Stair Falls was a longer walk, over half a mile, to return to the river. There, I turned to follow the bank downstream along the portage trail, marked with a sign reading "Stair Fall View."

Gazing back up at the rapid, I was struck by how different the character of each of the four falls had been. The splendid grandeur of Grand Pitch, charming little Pond Pitch, the fantastically strange Haskell Rock Pitch, and now aptly named Stair Falls, where eight ledges, varying in height from eight inches to two feet, descended in a perfect staircase.

On the bank above the stairs, I could see a red canoe pulled up on shore. According to my map, there was a campsite there, at the start of the portage.

The two men who belonged to the canoe soon came down the portage trail.

"Are you going to run Stair Falls?" I wondered, after we'd said hello.

"We're thinking about it. We have to look at the rest, but it actually looks pretty good."

The taller one, whose name was Johnson, seemed unworried about running the Class II+ rapid. I explained about my lighter Kevlar boat, and my plans to return in a few weeks to run the river. Their canoe was made of heavier, sturdier Royalex and belonged to the quieter of the two, Dana. With his dark hair and beard, he was one of those people who immediately remind you of someone you know.

After a couple of days of solitude, it was fun to have company. After we'd walked back up to the campsite, I plied them with questions, while they repacked some of their gear. Dana and Johnson had started their trip at Chamberlain Bridge and could give me an update on current river conditions. Before long, I'd offered to film their run down Stair Falls. Johnson was delighted.

"Don't worry! If you dump, I won't post it on Facebook," I reassured him. Looking back, this was rather an absurd comment, given the pair's level of experience. If I'd known where they worked, I would have known how easy they'd make it look.

Johnson just laughed, "If we dump, I really want it on Facebook."

Before I walked back down the portage trail to get in place, Johnson generously offered to send me his trip notes. To get them to me before my trip, he would have to type them up quickly, then email them to my father, to print out and bring to the Chamberlain Bridge resupply. When Johnson wrote down his email address, I noticed that he worked for the Chewonki Foundation, whose older campers undertake some very rigorous wilderness canoe trips. Later, I would discover that both men had been program leaders for Chewonki and, before that, New Hampshire's Camp Takodah, where they met.

River guidebooks generally recommend sticking to the center of the river in descending Stair Falls. Kellogg calls this rapid a light Class III with many possible routes. To me, it looked like there were many possible places to hang on the ledges. I got in place with my camera, knowing that my videography skills were novice at best and hoping that the focus would be clear.

The red canoe launched, then gradually grew larger in the frame. Dana was in the stern and Johnson, with his Indiana Jones hat, in the bow. They chose a straight, confident line, slightly right of center. Their strokes were calm and measured. Once, when the canoe threatened to turn sideways, Johnson's quick cross draw brought it back. One by one, the canoe passed safely through the whitewater lines marking each stair. Then, with a whoop and a wave, they passed me and were gone downstream.

I felt optimistic that the friends (whom I would come to know as "Goose" and "Maverick") would send those trip notes. Having an up-to-date report on conditions from Chamberlain Bridge to my takeout at Grindstone Falls would be fantastic. *How often help arrives unlooked-for*, I mused. Did faith or prayer lead to the providential crossing of our paths? Whether through faith or prayers or just our own attitude, I believe we play a part in those good happenings that my Grandma Jan always called serendipity.

Think about the chances. Two experienced river guides pause briefly for lunch, forty miles into their swift and capable navigation of the same waters that I would soon face. Meanwhile, I wind my slow way north, at a pace more reminiscent of the steadfast tortoise. We meet, at one of the few places where we could have. To me, this kind of thing happens too often to be pure chance.

Fondly remembering my grandmother and her serendipities, I turned away from the river and headed back to the IAT. The fun of scouting was over, and soon my backpacking adventure would be, too. Six miles of walking remained to reach the Matagamon Wilderness campground and store, where my parents were picking me up the following morning. I was still eager to see a moose. There had been so much moose sign, and I knew moose were often seen along the roads. Dreaming of moose, I walked on.

Entering the national monument from the north, the Messer Pond Road provides vehicle access to the Haskell Gate, less than two miles from Stair Falls. I would be hiking that route in reverse. At the gate, overnight parking is currently allowed with a free permit. When I turned north onto that road, only one lonely pickup truck was parked there on this sunny July day.

A half hour later, I could see a dark shape on the road ahead. I walked from the shade out into glaring sun, beside another abandoned beaver pond. In the wide sunlit opening, emerald grass sprouted from the rich soil surrounding a small pool, with a backdrop of hill and valley.

As I drew closer, the shape in the middle of the road became an angry, totally fearless snapping turtle, perhaps a late-nesting female. She circled defensively, then settled into position to stare me down. How primeval she looked, with her long curving dinosaur tail and rough, wrinkled skin. Thick moss grew on her shell, and her near hind foot was missing a claw.

I lay down on the road a safe distance away, where I could gaze into her eyes. Rays of amber radiated from a dark unblinking pupil. In a body that was all green moss and weathered brown skin, they shone bright. In those eyes were ninety million years of survival.

Eye to eye with a snapping turtle

Snapping turtles evolved in North America and have endured, relatively unchanged, since the time of the dinosaurs.

According to a March 2012 article in *Audubon Magazine*, by Ted Levin, snapping turtles are well-adapted to life in habitats like this former beaver pond. They hibernate almost half the year, "…dreaming turtle dreams tucked beneath a blanket of anoxic mud in the weedy, eutrophic shallows of ponds, marshes, and lakeshores, their pilot lights barely flickering. The ability to endure exposure to low levels of dissolved oxygen permits snapping turtles to winter in sites that are off-limits to wood turtles," one of the monument's less common turtle species.

About three and a half miles up the road from the Haskell Gate, a sign announced my imminent departure from the national monument. At just that moment, there was my moose. In the shadows ahead, on the left, a young bull was calmly strolling up the edge of the road ahead of me. Soon, he crossed into the sun, where I could see him better.

His fuzzy brown antlers stuck out horizontally, each with a small fork at the end. Later, I learned that a moose's antlers can grow an incredible one inch per day. His long, lanky legs carried him slowly up the road. He sauntered along, browsing the roadside brush. His speed was my speed, and I was content to enjoy this moment for as long as I could. At last, he faded into the thick young forest, and I went on.

A man had passed me earlier in a red pickup truck, the bed piled high with cut brush. An enthusiastic black Lab hung out of the passenger window, panting. On his way back, the driver leaned out to encourage me, "It's right over the top of the hill." He knew where I was headed.

Then he asked, "How did you find the trail?"

This, I thought, was an interesting choice of words. *How did I find the trail?* I had found it alternately picturesque and mundane, clear and confusing, tiring and rewarding. At times, I had barely found it at all. It was obvious, though, that much trail maintenance was being done by a core group of dedicated and hard-working volunteers. Thanks to them, I had experienced stunning 360-degree mountain views, met my share of wildlife, and been introduced to one of Maine's premier wild rivers. In the end, the International Appalachian Trail delivered me safely to civilization. From the turn onto Grand Lake Road, it was just a short walk across the bridge over the East Branch and into the campground.

At the camp store, I met owners Sue and Joe Christianson and their daughter, Katie. I didn't know it at the time, but I should have guessed. Here was another family who would offer me not only a warm welcome, but hospitality, help, and friendship when I needed it most.

There were several available campsites. I chose one right on the river and as close as I could be to the showers and, of course, Mama Bears' Kitchen. I had big plans for that, beginning with a bacon cheeseburger for dinner. The restaurant served pizza, burgers, and sandwiches, as well as breakfast in the morning. The well-stocked store carried nonperishable and refrigerated groceries, camping and fishing supplies, and even books.

I took advantage of the Wi-Fi to catch up on the news while I ate. At my elbow, stretching along one wall, was an amazingly life-like scene. Five black bears stood among rocks and branches, along with a raccoon, ruffed grouse, and whitetail buck. In the morning, I came back for French toast and bacon, coffee and orange juice, which I ate while I caught up on my journal. I got to talking with Sue about my first book, *Upwards*, which by the end of the day was for sale in the store.

Joe patiently answered my questions about river conditions. He helps operate the Matagamon Dam, which releases water into the East Branch. Lake levels were currently being lowered to do repair work on the bridge and dam. The dam had been releasing water at 650 cubic feet per second two weeks ago, was now at 500, and would be releasing at much lower levels, perhaps 150 to 200, in two or three weeks. This was concerning news, as the river might look very different from what I had just observed.

By late morning, my gear was dry and packed, ready to load in the truck when Mom and Dad arrived a short time later. I brought in Sue's book order from the truck, introduced everybody, and got a photo with my new friends before we headed for home. For a few days, I would rest and reorganize my gear and thoughts, to prepare for the more challenging canoeing part of my adventure.

E–Ledge on the West Branch, where darkness forced my first stealth camp

Canada lilies and swamp milkweed brighten the river shore

Evening falls over the Canvas Dam campsite on Caucomgomoc Stream

Nothing was going to interrupt her lunch

The map comes to life—Allagash Lake from the top of the fire tower

Safely across Allagash Lake

Lesser purple fringed bog orchid

Windy afternoon on Chamberlain Lake

Mom and Dad resupply me at Chamberlain Bridge

Katahdin from a Loop Road overlook in the national monument

First look at the East Branch from the Whetstone Bridge

Goose and Maverick running Stair Falls

Young bull moose in the monument

With new friends Joe and Sue Christianson

Trying to keep up with Mama on the shores of Webster Lake

Sunset one enchanted evening

Webster Brook meets the East Branch

*Classic Maurice "Jake" Day painting of Ed and Mary
Smith's camp on Grand Lake Matagamon*

The calm before the chaos on the upper East Branch

Morning mist rising over Pond Pitch

Female belted kingfisher

Cardinal flower

Silver maples overhang tranquil Lunksoos Deadwater

PART III

THE CANOE TRIP

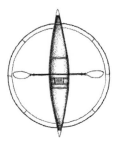

CHAPTER 10

AN ENCHANTED EVENING

Still they stood,
A great wave from it going over them,
As if the earth in one unlooked-for favour,
Had made them certain earth returned their love.

—**Robert Frost**, *"Two Look at Two"*

Two weeks later, I bent over the canoe at the Chamberlain Bridge boat landing, placing each dry bag in its proper spot. It was a bittersweet moment. This canoe trip I had dreamed up was more than halfway finished, and it was time to journey on. I was rested, resupplied, and ready for the final lap to the national monument. Once more, I said good-bye and turned my back on family to face the unknown ahead.

The Allagash has a ridiculous number of small bodies of water named Round Pond, including one on the north end of Telos. In the first three-quarters of an hour, I struggled down its short length to the lake proper, where the full force of the wind was revealed. It was intense, sometimes battling me to a standstill, as I dug in hard just to hold the boat steady. *Don't fight its power*, I thought, *don't lose ground, just be patient.* The gusts were as strong or stronger than those the previous day on Chamberlain Lake.

The stunning scenery stood in sharp contrast to the elemental power of the wind.

This was a gorgeous lake of layers. Sun highlighted the lower shore, where blotches of bright-green hardwood mingled in among darker evergreens. Down the lake, the waves of forest rose to meet the peaks of distant Baxter State Park. Nature had painted the ridges countless shades of blue, with nuances of clarity as well as hue. High above, clouds dashed across a sky of sapphire, its brightness so different from the roiled darkness of the water.

For a time, the western shore curved gradually inward, offering some protection from the wind. I made progress, very slowly. An hour and a half after entering Telos, I had gone less than a mile.

Ahead lay a small point. As I pushed around it, fully exposed to the south now, my weary muscles began to rebel. I fought, determined to hold steady, and felt the waves driving the canoe toward shore. I was losing control. The wind forced me relentlessly toward the gravel beach, which was guarded by a maze of sharp rocks. It was too shallow to maneuver and too dangerous to simply wait. Abruptly, I felt fear and knew I had to get my canoe out of the water. These are the moments when a flashing thought reminds you that you are miles from help, in weather that would keep most people in camp.

I aimed for the shelter of a huge rock. Shielded from the grasp of the pounding waves. I climbed out and worked the canoe toward the beach. In the end, I had to unload the boat, balancing my dry bags precariously on the wet and slippery rocks, while keeping a firm hand on the canoe. Load by awkward load, I carried gear and boat to the edge of the woods, where I tied up the canoe and sat down to think.

My evening plans were already dashed. Straight across the lake was a splendid site called High Bank, at which I'd intended to stay. In these conditions, though, I knew that there would be no crossing the lake. Telos had only one other official campsite, more than five miles ahead. I could reach it by following this shore to the quiet, sheltered southern end of the lake. If I could get there.

Luckily, there was no one around to see me. I stumbled along the beach, hauling my dry bags, heavy with the weight of all that added food. Carrying the boat, I held on tightly, while the wind threatened to wrench it from my grasp. A little over a tenth of a mile and everything was around the point and tucked safely behind a giant downed tree.

Then I rested, my back against a dry and shaded rock, and wrote: *Curling whitecaps race in mighty legions, as the heads of marsh grass bow. Water, churned coffee brown, breaks on shore in rolling waves, but the distant mountains in their blue haze are unmoved. They know that calm will follow frenzy, as it has done since the birthing of this lake. This one lesson we come to learn, that there are many things beyond our understanding, or our control. The Penobscot knew this. Perhaps they, too, rested here, immersed in beauty, and thought great thoughts, thanked the Creator, and simply waited. For the wind will calm, sometime, we have only to wait.*

Around four o'clock, imagining a slight lull, I commenced a two-hour, three-mile push to the southwest corner of the lake. The shallows there were full of spatterdock, another distinctive native aquatic plant. The vivid dots of yellow brought back the memory of an early morning camp, years ago, on Fish Pond near Jackman. A moose had come out to keep me company across a small cove, feeding among a bounty of yellow water lilies, whose name I didn't then know. She glanced my way, seeming to accept my quiet presence. Later, after she had gone, I paddled over to study the flowers more closely.

Spatterdock, also called cow lily, has a large, floating oval heart-shaped leaf with a small notch at the base. Its distinctive yellow, ball-shaped flower is encircled by a layer of tightly wrapped petals. Within is a yellow circle with rays like a little sun. When the fruit matures, the flower transforms into a deep maroon vase-shaped fruit with touches of green.

If the cow I'd been watching that morning was feeding a calf or two, she would have needed to eat an amazing sixty-six pounds of food daily, the highest nutritional need of any moose. Moose browse year-round on the leaves, needles, and twigs of hardwood and balsam fir, which provide the bulk of their diet. In the warmer months, aquatic plants like water lilies and pondweed become a valuable food source, providing crucial sodium. Waterfowl, deer, muskrat, beaver. and porcupine also dine on spatterdock.

There had been moments on Telos when I'd been certain that I would have to spend the night on a lonely beach beside the thick, dark forest. Instead, with a lighter heart, I went east along the protected south shore, through relatively quiet water. After several miles, the lake narrowed. The last official campsite, Murphy's Field, was close now, straight across on the north shore.

I was almost home for the night.

As I angled away from shore, a loon called from somewhere near, and almost immediately, I could feel the wind return. Of course, it had been there all along, a fact that never ceases to surprise you when you leave some sheltered spot for open water. I found the campsite and hauled everything up into a clearing encircled by stately white pine. The wind ruled out a campfire. Later, I snuggled into my sleeping bag as darkness fell. The thin fabric of the tent shook and flapped, and I thought warily of the mighty pines above my head.

Thankfully, no trees fell in the night, although the wind never let up. By five I was up, in light rain, glad that I'd brought most of my stuff inside the protection of the tent. I made a cup of double-strength coffee under the vestibule and ate a trail bar, meanwhile carefully re-packing to keep everything as dry as possible. I left a note for the rangers on the picnic table, pinned down by a large rock, in case they cruised down to see if I'd made it safely. By six-thirty, I was on my way, ready to race the rain through Telos Cut to my lean-to at the far end of Webster Lake.

In the end, I almost won.

Peace infused that early hour. A family of mergansers stayed with me along the shore, and I was alert for bear or mink, bobcat or lynx. The wind, gentle now, nudged me along. For two miles, I followed the last narrow arm of the lake northeast toward Telos Dam.

Not the grandest of structures, this remote dam nonetheless has great historical and geological significance and continues to impact both the Allagash/St. John and East Branch/Penobscot drainages.

Nature, of course, was the first to shape and reshape Maine's landscape and resulting watersheds. The backbone of the Appalachian Mountains has dictated the direction of flow of the major rivers of this region for hundreds of millions of years. On one side, the Allagash flows north into the St. John River, headed for Canada, a turn to the south, and ultimately the Bay of Fundy. On the other side, the East Branch flows south into the Penobscot River and ultimately Penobscot Bay.

Just a short time ago in the scope of Earth's history, another force sculpted the landscape. During the last couple of million years, geologists believe several glaciers advanced and retreated across Maine. The Laurentide Ice Sheet, the most recent, was several thousand feet thick, and its sheer weight depressed the land several hundred feet. It scraped and eroded bedrock, moved boulders as heavy as eight thousand tons, and deposited sediments, creating features like the esker I'd hiked along on the IAT.

Lastly came man, sometimes making changes as sweeping as those of nature. Construction of the original Telos Dam, begun in 1840, was the first move of a pawn in a masterful game of chess that would ultimately change the direction of rivers and bring vast quantities of Allagash timber south.

At that time, the city of Bangor, on the Penobscot River below the junction of the East and West Branches, was the undisputed lumber capital of the world. White pine was the premier species being harvested, not just for the famed ship masts, but for lumber in all shapes and sizes. To keep the mills supplied, lumber barons looked farther and farther upstream along the rivers that fed the Penobscot.

In the Allagash, there was plenty of white pine, but no rivers flowing south toward Bangor.

"The Strickland Brothers and Amos Roberts owned Township 6, Range 11 (half of Webster Lake and all of Telos)," writes Gil Gilpatrick in *Allagash: A Journey Through Time on Maine's Legendary Wilderness Waterway*. In 1839, they were harvesting pine around Webster Lake that they hoped to drive down through Webster Brook toward the Penobscot. "One has to understand that these men were doers, not dreamers. The fact that there would be insufficient water from little Webster Lake to make a successful drive down the brook did not deter them from going ahead with their cutting operation. They would worry about the water problem when the time came."

The Stricklands and Roberts hired lumberman and engineer Shepard Boody to survey the area and come up with a plan. He discovered that, from the shore of Telos Lake, the elevation rose just five or six feet over a tenth of a mile to the height of land, then dropped gradually away for about the same distance. From there, a natural gully descended forty-seven feet over a mile to Webster Lake. This ravine, most likely carved by a glacier, was the obvious solution.

By 1841, two dams were in place—one at the height of land just beyond Telos and another at the outlet of Chamberlain Lake, where Lock Dam stands today. Together, they would contain and redirect the Chamberlain Lake waters, increasing the area of the East Branch watershed by approximately 25 percent. That same year, a canal was dug from Telos to the height of land and the ravine cleared to create what is now called Telos Cut. In 1842, the first Allagash pine was driven through the cut and down the East Branch to the hungry Bangor mills.

As an added benefit, these logs were no longer subject to the duties owed to Great Britain on timber run down the St. John and shipped through Canadian ports. Later, however, there was another controversial chapter in the story. Bangor lumberman Rufus Dwinel purchased the township and promptly set a high toll on logs run through Telos Cut. Before the Maine State Legislature stepped in to resolve the dispute, the "Telos War" almost came to bloodshed.

To enforce his unpopular toll, Dwinel hired seventy-five "Bangor Tigers," reputedly the toughest of the log-driving rivermen. "He brought them to his dam armed with knives, picks, handpikes, and axes," writes Gilpatrick. "These fellows were more accustomed to brawling with fists, teeth, and spiked boots, but they were willing and eager to wield their new weapons in defense of their employer's property."

The tolls were paid, but then the war moved on to the legislature. Ultimately, Dwinel agreed to a fair toll and was granted an official state charter to operate the dam, ending the conflict.

As I approached the dam, I thought of the many layers of history that would surround my trip through Telos Cut and beyond. Ahead, a geometric pattern of wood and metal gradually took shape, its man-made outline a bit of a shock in this untamed setting. A large wooden sign warned, "DANGER. STRONG CURRENTS NEAR DAM. ALL PARTIES TAKE OUT ON RIGHT."

Approaching Telos Dam (above) and view from the top, looking down Telos Cut

This timber crib structure, a newer dam dating to the 1980s, is currently operated by the Allagash Wilderness Waterway for fisheries management and recreation. The waters of Chamberlain and Telos now flow into both watersheds, through Lock Dam into Eagle Lake and the Allagash and through Telos Dam into Webster Lake and the Penobscot.

Today, I would benefit from increased water flows. When I'd met Ben on Allagash Stream, the ranger explained that he'd just opened Telos dam to 236 cfs to drop the level of Chamberlain Lake for repairs to Lock Dam. Gazing down from the top of the dam, my eyes followed the swift water as it swept straight away between thickly wooded banks, before turning out of sight.

Thoreau and his friend Hoar had walked this mile, carrying "the greater part of the baggage," while Joe Polis, their Penobscot guide, ran the cut alone in his birchbark canoe. I was hoping to run part of it. According to Ben, I could put in about halfway down, after the worst of the rapids.

To start, I carried all my gear the length of the carry, leaving my canoe at the dam. Though the trail was mostly dry and pleasant, there were some rocky and muddy spots, plus a huge downed tree to lift over. The glimpses I had of the upper stream were of vigorous, rocky whitewater.

How had my new friends Johnson Whippie, "Goose," and Dana Cinq-Mars, "Maverick," fared here? They'd camped their first night at High Bank, after encountering a very different Telos Lake. "We were met by a pristine golden hour of sunset illuminating our views of Katahdin as we paddled across the glassy surface, leaving only gentle ripples for the passing loons to notice us by," Goose recalled.

Not unexpectedly, given their whitewater expertise, they'd run all of Telos Cut the next morning, calling the stretch "entertaining" in their Royalex boat. "We scraped on a number of shallow spots and ran completely aground once as well. We scouted the first one-quarter mile of this to determine we felt comfortable playing it as a read and run river." They did add that, at lower water or in a nicer boat, they might have made a different decision.

Walking back toward the dam after depositing my gear, I munched on an apple and searched for the spot where Ben had said

I could put in. About halfway back, a faint path, wide enough for the canoe, led down through the woods to the water. Downstream, the water deepened, with strong current, but no rapids. I left my hat on the trail to mark the spot and retrieved my boat. That last section turned out to be a fun paddle, with just a few small standing waves—stationary, predictable waves that occur where fast water meets slower water or an underwater obstacle. I soon reached the spot where I'd stashed my gear.

Somewhere near the middle of three-mile-long Webster Lake, I entered Baxter State Park. My camping reservations for the next two nights had been made months ago, for a total cost of $42. The park utilizes a four-month rolling window, meaning that reservations for a specific date open exactly four months earlier. That had been a good incentive to put firm dates in my calendar by the end of March.

I hugged the south shore, following a pair of spotted sandpipers, their darting the only movement in a gray world. Clouds and mist hung low over the lake. My paddle sliced the water in steady rhythm, no louder than the patter of the rain. It was at once beautiful, serene, and lonely. A shiver of wildness ran through me, birthed by craggy humps of ancient rock, the deep mist-enshrouded forest, and the haunting echo of loon voices. As if to match my mood, the rain grew in intensity, gaining energy and force. I paddled on.

The Webster Outlet lean-to is at the far end of the lake, near the start of Webster Brook.

"I don't want a mousey lean-to," I remembered telling the helpful woman who had taken my reservation, months before. "I like to sleep in my tent," I'd added firmly. She had assured me that there was plenty of room near the lean-to for camping.

Well, that small and cozy lean-to, perhaps eight feet by ten feet, looked mighty good. Once my canoe was stowed well up on shore, I changed into dry, warm clothes and sat under the shelter of the moss-covered roof, looking out over the water. It seemed likely that no one else would come this way today. For an afternoon, this vista of woods and waters was mine.

By now, I had paddled off the edge of NFCT Map 12. I spread the map out to dry, so I could put it away. With the rest of my gear dripping from nails and hooks and the ends of the logs, I sat down to

A cozy haven on a damp day

study the route ahead. It was comforting to read that the difficult rapids ahead all had portage trails, if caution urged me off the river. With eternal optimism, I prayed that this time I would find them.

Nearly thirty thousand acres in this northwest corner of Baxter State Park are designated as the SFMA or Scientific Forest Management Area. This area is open to hunting and trapping, except for moose hunting and hunting over bait. Former Maine Governor and park founder Percival P. Baxter envisioned the SFMA as "a show place for those interested in forestry, a place where a continuing timber crop can be cultivated, harvested, and sold; where reforestation and scientific cutting will be employed; an example and an inspiration to others."

"What is done in our forests today will help or harm the generations who follow us," Baxter continued. All proceeds from SFMA timber sales are held in trust to be used solely for the care, management, and protection of the park.

Around one o'clock, I watched the fog creep ever closer, drawing in the walls of my visible world. No, not fog, I realized, but a wall of light rain. The nearest island, not far away, became a foggy outline of its true self. Floating on a sea of white, its outline of rocky cliffs crowned with trees was just a fuzzy gray-green blur. On the nearest shore, dark silhouettes of conifers stood to attention in a long row that faded away into nothing.

Thoreau, in *The Maine Woods*, writes, "If I wished to see a mountain or other scenery under the most favorable auspices, I would go to it in foul weather, so as to be there when it cleared up; we are then in the most suitable mood, and nature is most fresh and inspiring. There is no serenity so fair as that which is just established in a tearful eye."

In late afternoon, the weather cleared for a magic hour.

The canoe drew me down to the water's edge. I glided silently out into the stillness, feeling light and unencumbered. Along the north shore, I discovered a spot where both red and jack pines grew. Both species are shorter, with thicker needles and smaller cones, than the more common eastern white pine (*Pinus strobus*). The ubiquitous white pine, which often reaches one hundred feet in height, has dainty white-lined needles, three to five inches long, in bundles of five. Its elegant, though often pitch-covered, cones are four to eight inches long.

Red pine (*Pinus resinosa*), named for its distinctive reddish-brown bark and pale red heartwood, can grow to eighty feet tall. I've often found stands of red pine on rocky bluffs along northern Maine lakeshores. It has four to six-inch-long needles, in bundles of two. The cones of red pine are about two inches long and regular in shape.

Jack pine (*Pinus banksiana*) is noticeably shorter, only infrequently growing to a height of fifty or sixty feet. Although they also occur in clusters of two, jack pine needles are much shorter, less than two inches long, and twisted. The small curved cones have a unique characteristic. They are serotinous, opening most efficiently when the intense heat of a wildfire triggers seed release.

I crossed the lake to the far shore. Some way ahead, the thick forest gave way to the windings of a small brook, overhung with brushy alder, which emerged from a wide area of dead standing timber. From that direction, a doe and spotted fawn appeared. They moved briskly in my direction, the fawn trotting to keep up with momma, who paused just once or twice along the way to drink. His tail waved and his knees lifted high. Each time she stopped, the fawn nuzzled her, as if to say, "Still here!" The baby was a richer brown, his spots clean white in the lighting of the almost-sun.

I sat in my canoe, motionless, perhaps a hundred feet from shore. Certainly, I should have been visible to them. A yellow canoe, the only object on the calm mirror of water. Yet they came on, until they were almost even with me, the doe stopping now to gaze right at this strange object on her lake. Deep brown eyes, big ears, the light glowing through them as an almost translucent pink. She looked more inquisitive than wary, and I thought of Robert Frost's poem, "Two Look at Two."

When mother and baby at last walked quietly away into the woods, the calm endured.

Thoughts of Webster Lake, I know, will always bring memories of this enchanted evening, long after I can come no more. Back at camp, the rain resumed until, around eight o'clock, it stopped for good. I could finally have a campfire, aided by copious amounts of birch bark and dead fir branches to encourage the reluctant flames. A couple of garter snakes hung around camp, and the fire kept me company, too. It seemed almost alive as it crackled and danced.

To the west, the sun finally won through a line of clouds to reflect on the evening-dark waters, a subtle, tranquil ending to a day of unexpected blessings.

But, no, I turned again, and the sky had exploded in a blaze of apocalyptic color, perhaps beyond the craft of words to capture. From two angles, like giant spotlights, the yellow-orange ember glow of the setting sun shone up upon billowing towers of cloud, purple-gray in the shadows. Below the black silhouette of treetops, two wide paths of coral light shimmered across the water toward camp.

At that moment, a barred owl began to call from deep in the forest, the notes finding their way straight into my soul.

CHAPTER 11

THE RUSH OF A LITTLE BROOK

This Webster Stream is well known to lumbermen as a difficult one. It is exceedingly rapid and rocky, and also shallow, and can hardly be considered navigable, unless that may mean that what is launched in it is sure to be carried swiftly down it, though it may be dashed to pieces by the way. It is somewhat like navigating a thunder-spout.

—Henry David Thoreau, *The Maine Woods*

The shelter did have mice, or at least one mouse! As usual, the bags of food and cooking gear were outside, dangling from a high branch. Inside the lean-to, I'd hung my tent awkwardly from a few existing nails. I'd wiggled in, then zipped the zippers tightly closed. I really don't like the thought of mice scampering over me while I'm asleep.

In the depths of the night, I woke to movement. Something had run across the thin nylon of the tent, and then the clear silhouette of a mouse stood frozen for a moment against the netting. Ugh!

Sleep returned, and by morning, the charm of the lake was restored, making me wish I didn't have to say farewell. I lingered over breakfast, cramming my mind full of the details of descending nearby Webster Brook. By night, if all went well, I would be camped where Webster Brook enters the East Branch, just above Grand Lake Matagamon.

To guide me, there were a few sentences in the AMC river guide and a detailed narrative and map in Zip Kellogg's booklet, originally published by DeLorme in 1983. Much could have changed in thirty-five years. In addition, I wondered if my interpretation of phrases like *sheer entertainment* and *very small drop* might differ from that of the author, who was an accomplished whitewater paddler.

Water levels were on the low side of ideal. The previous day's rain and recent opening of Telos Dam would help, bringing the flow closer to the recommended threshold of 300 cubic feet per second.

All agreed that the challenge ahead could be tackled in stages.

First, three miles of strong Class II rapids, which I planned to run. Second, a respite—three slower miles, where the stream takes a meditative breath, a magical place of flowery islands and quiet beaches. Lastly, chaos—nearly four miles, beginning before difficult Class III Indian Carry, then continuing through two miles of exhilarating whitewater to Grand Pitch, which everyone portages.

Even Goose and Maverick.

I determined to worry about one stage at a time.

My new friends had been delighted with the first segment. "It was really fun meandering read-and-run Class I rapids. We lost ourselves in the fun of the winding river and *very* quickly made our way to nearly the trail junction for Hudson Pond. The sides of the river are riddled with strainers but very few were hazardous to a paddler's journey and thanks to our handsaw there are even fewer now!"

I took heart from Goose and Maverick's rating of this section as Class I. At quarter to nine on a sunny, cool, breezy morning, I clipped everything in, zipped my head net safely in a PFD pocket, and pulled my way through the rocky, shallow remains of another old log driving dam. An osprey soared high above, and I tried to guess which rock had once been Thoreau's dining table. Then Webster Brook lay before me, vigorous, beckoning, lifting my heart and my pulse.

The thrills started without delay. Scouting carefully at first, I progressed only a half-mile in the first half hour. The black flies were out in full force, and I sprayed myself with abandon.

Gradually, my confidence grew. Upper Webster Brook embodied all that was best in a lively little northern river. Rapids that could mostly be run on the fly, fast current, wild shores where the fir and spruce reached skyward. Once, I startled a deer in little hidden cove on river left. With a mighty lunging whoosh of tail and hindquarters in a blurry arch, he or she was gone.

Twice I paused to rest and write. *Wow, it feels like I've done Chase Rapids plus. The water still seems low, and there are some mighty rocks. My hands are shaking. I'm sitting on an island above a classic strainer, a huge downed white pine stretching out into the channel, with current sweeping through it. The river bends and I cannot see what lies ahead.* Farther along, I wrote again, a dragonfly perched daintily upon my knee. *So much is crammed into mere hours that I've worried about for so long. What a rush! After running a long stretch, I am stopping in the shade to let my heart rate drop.*

I was close to Hudson Brook and the start of calmer waters, when I came the closest to dumping. The canoe hung up on an unseen rock, amid a strong Class II rapid, and wouldn't budge. As the current strained to turn the boat sideways, I hopped out, anchoring myself firmly against the rock. I wrestled the boat free and worked it around until it faced downstream. Paddle at the ready, I jumped in, and shot away, still surprisingly dry. Two and a half hours had passed since I'd said farewell to Webster Lake.

Then, abruptly, the character of the river changed. I had safely reached the second leg.

In the slow current, the boat went lightly along, and I soaked in all there was to see. So many worlds—down through sun-drenched water, clear but for a tiny waver, to the dart and dash of minnows among the rocks. Past flowery banks of bright pastels that opened now and then into hidden places, just a glimpse before I drifted past, like the quiet courtyards of a southern city behind brick and iron walls.

Goose and Maverick had camped within these peaceful meanders, on a lovely island they called Bear Haven, "in honor of the bear we displaced from munching on it." It had "strawberry banks" and a sandy area where they swam and napped. They were glad they had embraced the "find the next enticing location to stop" mentality. Continuing downstream the following day, they did not discover many suitable camping spots below Bear Haven.

Although Thoreau and Hoar missed most of the excitement of Webster Brook, they did join Joe Polis on the river for this serene interlude. I was glad they hadn't missed this. The upper rapids had been truly fun—not a chore—but this was blissful. There were stately Canada lilies and a bald eagle that rose on powerful wings to cross above my head. Quickwater alternated with gentle curves, where the water deepened. Once, I came upon a merganser with little ones. These were the birds Thoreau called *sheldrakes*, and their behavior today mirrored what he had often observed. The mother and three young scurried along, heads straining urgently forward, bodies churning the surface like a kids' water battle.

About six miles from Webster Lake, the river awoke once more. I filtered water beside the first small ledge drop that signaled a change was coming. On the upper rocks, where it was dry, I stretched out, leaning back on the soft cushion of my PFD to eat my lunch. The rippled muscles of rock were traced with green and orange moss and lichens. On the air was the tangy taste of fir. The ledge slipped down into the stream and across. The water came from upstream as a smooth curtain of green, then dropped over the ledge into frothy white and surged forward toward the mysteries that lay downstream.

Not far ahead was the former site of the Indian Carry lean-to, which is referenced in Kellogg's narrative as a landmark visible along the right bank. However, thanks to Goose and Maverick, I knew the lean-to could no longer be found. These days, its location is obscured by blow downs and understory growth, if indeed it still exists.

According to Kellogg, upcoming Indian Carry demands "strong strokes" and "technical maneuvering" and should probably only be run by experienced paddlers. I would walk the portage trail on river right. "Although the Indians carried their canoes around this pitch," Kellogg explains, "the name is a misnomer here. The Indians would have portaged much of Webster Brook, in fact, because prior to 1841 it was a smaller, rockier, but still a steep stream." He refers, of course, to the impact of Telos Dam.

Wowzer! Thus, began Goose and Maverick's description of the third part of the Webster Brook descent, from Indian Carry to the imposing Grand Pitch, some two miles farther downstream. Goose somehow also managed to use the word *fun* several times.

"This stretch is *really* fun," he enthused. A hard-to-miss horizon line across the width of the river marked the start of the excitement.

"We found the next stretch of river super fun and engaging for a boat that was looking for fun drops," he continued, adding that scouting for the best lines was often advisable. "With participants or with a Kevlar boat, some drops may be deemed too scrapy. We hardly left any paint on rocks in this stretch as the water flow was just right and the lines were perfect for us."

After lining my canoe around my lunchtime ledge, I continued cautiously downriver, trying my best to match what I was seeing to Kellogg's directions. To find the start of Indian Carry, I was looking for two "very small drops." The second would come after one sloping, evergreen-crowned ledge on the left bank and before another one, which jutted out into the stream across from the take-out.

I was not Goose or Maverick. It would not be prudent to simply wait until I saw an unmistakable horizon line stretching from bank to bank. By then, I might be past the start of the portage trail.

Do you know how many ledges and evergreen-crowned banks this little river has? I thought.

Twice more, I was forced to unload and line the empty canoe down through rapids. I began looking for the portage trail too early, due to the overwhelming abundance of ledges and evergreen crowns. After exploring for a while along the Freezeout Trail, which hugged the right bank, I finally oriented myself and found the obvious start of the well-marked Indian Carry portage. There were several options for taking out, all on river right, across from a high cliff topped with tall conifers.

By the time I finished the one-tenth-mile portage, it was mid-afternoon. Two miles of river remained before the mandatory Grand Pitch portage. Crazy or not, I hoped to run some of it.

Neither the AMC river guide nor Kellogg were very encouraging. The former describes several very difficult Class III ledge drops through this section, best run by experts. Kellogg cites the names of four of them, which never bodes well for the cautious. *Big Woodpecker, Little Woodpecker, the Cow Yard,* and *Blue Pine*—these intriguing, and perhaps almost forgotten, names come from a 1939 article in the popular Bangor & Aroostook Railroad publication, *In the Maine Woods.* The route described in the magazine largely mirrored mine but began at the south end of Moosehead Lake and followed Mud

Pond Carry into the Allagash, through "wild untrammeled country, spired by the up-flung peaks of the Katahdin Range." Along this stretch of Webster Brook, clients could expect to walk, while the bad pitches would require "some tall and fancy work on the part of the guide."

"Webster Brook is narrow through this section," Kellogg continues, "so the standing waves at these pitches can be sizable. Scout or portage any of them on the right if it seems necessary. The pitches are separated from each other by gentle water."

I had just begun to portage the first of the four, Big Woodpecker, when the thunder that had been rumbling in the distance began to crack almost overhead. I knew I was going to get wet. After scrambling to finish the short portage, I leaned the canoe against a thick tree trunk just above the final descent back to the river. The bags all fit nicely underneath.

Then, as the rain came in earnest, I saw the overturned canoe with its tidy row of bags anew. Quickly, I scooted around to the far side, where the canoe lay tipped against the tree, and crawled underneath. Wiggling and shifting a bit, I made myself comfortable on a bed of gear as the skies let loose.

For a full half hour, I rested. The storm's thunder grew louder and the lightning closer. Only my arm, which couldn't quite fit, felt the wind and the pelting of the ice-cold rain. The bugs had fled somewhere else, and I was surprisingly comfortable. My mind wandered, from past to present and back, thinking at last of Percival Proctor Baxter, once the state's governor, whose tenacity and generosity had eventually secured this lively brook, and much more, for the people of Maine.

The decades of efforts to protect Katahdin and environs within the boundaries of a state or national park or forest reserve could fill several chapters of a large book. Indeed, they do. *Legacy of a Lifetime: The Story of Baxter State Park*, by Dr. John W. Hakola, was commissioned by the Baxter State Park Authority and published to commemorate the park's fiftieth anniversary in 1981. I am indebted to this comprehensive work, as well as to *Katahdin, An Historic Journey,* by John W. Neff, for my discussions of the history of Baxter State Park.

By the late nineteenth and early twentieth centuries, a growing number of voices were calling for the protection of Maine's forests, fish, and game, particularly in the Katahdin area. The Maine Hotel Proprietor's Association, the *Bangor Daily Commercial,* and the Maine State Federation of Women's Clubs were all supporters of state conservation of the mountain.

An early bill, introduced by US Representative Frank E. Guernsey of Dover-Foxcroft and supported by the 1913 Maine State Legislature, would have created a national park and forest reserve around Katahdin. The Maine Sportsmen's Fish and Game Association and the Commissioners of Inland Fisheries and Game also spoke out in favor of the bill. However, it failed to pass.

By 1916, the leading voice for preservation of the area was newly elected State Representative Percival Proctor Baxter of Portland. The son of a wealthy family with interests in canning, transportation, real estate, and banking, Percival had always been extremely close to his father, James Phinney Baxter.

Percival's father was a multi-faceted person. A writer and historian, as well as a businessman, he once spent two years in France and England doing historical research on the colonial era. Later, he served six terms as mayor of Portland. Throughout his life, he set an example of philanthropy, founding public libraries and supporting city beautification, building, and land preservation, no doubt inspiring his son. Most importantly for our story, James was a passionate trout fisherman who made frequent trips to the wilds of Maine, often bringing along some of his children. It was in his father's company that Percy, as he was often called, first saw Katahdin up close, on a 1903 excursion to Kidney Pond.

"Many of the father's interests and accomplishments were later reflected in the son's life," writes Neff, "a love of the outdoors, a compelling commitment to public service, a desire to travel, an interest in history, and a dedication to using his own personal wealth for the benefit of the people of Maine."

Throughout his political career, Baxter often faced strong opposition because of his unwavering stance on water rights and public lands. He opposed the export of power from the state and favored repurchasing large tracts of burned or cutover land that had previously been sold away to the railroads and timber companies. This land, Baxter believed, should be reforested and held to ensure forest resources for the future. He angered paper companies, power companies, and political opponents alike. As his dream of creating Baxter State Park took hold and became his life's passion, he faced an uphill battle because of this long history of political controversy.

In 1919, as a state representative, Baxter introduced a bill that would have allowed for the purchase of land to create state parks and forest reserves around Katahdin and elsewhere in the state. The proposed legislation included an appropriation of $10,000 for each of the years 1919 and 1920, to buy land. Perhaps because the land could be obtained by eminent domain, the measure was strongly opposed by the powerful Great Northern Paper Company. The bill did not pass. However, another new law, allowing for the acceptance of gifts of land for state parks and forests, was enacted. Years later, it would provide the mechanism for Baxter State Park to be created in an entirely different way.

In 1920, Baxter entered the race for a Maine Senate seat. During the campaign, he promised to pursue his beloved state park as a memorial in honor of Maine's centennial year. Baxter won the election and quickly became president of the senate. From this position of power, and with increasing support, Baxter led the way in drafting a bill to establish Mount Katahdin State Park. The proposed legislation included an appropriation of $100,000 over two years for purchasing land and authorized its taking by eminent domain, for roads, trails, rights of way, and campsites.

This time, the measure seemed destined to pass.

As the thunderstorm retreated, I pulled my thoughts away from Baxter, whose story was far from over. I knew I must go on, quickly, or darkness would find me once again short of camp. I put back in, running rapids without a question that would have made me hesitate just hours before. I even ran one of the four big ones, on river left. All the while, the thunder continued its distant muttering, and I ignored it.

Some of the details are blurry now. There are few photos of this stretch.

At a point that I thought must be the beginning of the mandatory Grand Pitch portage, I started off down the portage trail, leaving my canoe for the second trip. The weight of the backpack bag felt heavier now, and I shifted the other bags from hand to hand to give my sore muscles a rest. After walking close to a half-mile, I got good news and bad. The good news was that I now knew for sure where I was. The bad news was that I had just dumped my pile of stuff at the start of the Grand Pitch portage, not the end.

Energy on such a day comes as you need it. Racing the dark is a powerful motivator, and soon the canoe had joined my gear beneath the sign. I was able to paddle the canoe for the last couple of tenths of this stretch. I decided to move forward, carrying the gear first again. I would scout out the trail, walking all the way to tonight's campsite, to see once and for all what was left to accomplish.

From the well-maintained trail, I marveled at the glimpses of whitewater I could see through the trees. Here was Thoreau's thunder-spout in all its glory. About halfway along, the current slowed dramatically. I left my bags on the bank, near the spot where the river settled down. Empty-handed, I scouted the rest of the trail, a mile in all from the sign to the campsite and its adjacent lean-to.

Thoreau had scrambled across a remarkably different landscape. In 1857, this area had been recently burned over, providing a clear view of the underlying rock. A series of high, narrow ridges ran in parallel, separated in places by deep ravines. Thoreau crossed one of these on the trunk of a huge, rotten pine tree, on which he found the fresh tracks of a moose. Great fields of fireweed covered the land in brilliant pink bloom, "the most extensive" that Thoreau had ever seen.

Observant as always, Thoreau noted the similarity in shape and orientation of these "great rock-waves" or "breakers." Taking out his compass, he discovered that they ran in a northwest–southeast direction. The one on which he stood rose to a height of eighty feet, with "an abrupt precipice" to the northeast, facing the river. The massive rock, a third of a mile long, lay on its edge, and the narrow ridgetop was only one to four feet wide. "No wonder that the river that found its way through them was rapid and obstructed by falls," Thoreau concluded.

It was almost seven, the sun low on the horizon, when I turned back to get the canoe for the final carry and paddle to camp. *This brook*, I thought, *deserves every adjective ever given to it, except perhaps fun!* That night, a zombie did the camp chores on willpower alone. The tent went up—there would be no mice tonight. Too exhausted to celebrate my accomplishment, I snuggled into my sleeping bag and drifted away without another thought.

CHAPTER 12

LOSING A GRAND LAKE

*The morning was a bright one, and perfectly still and serene, the
lake as smooth as glass, we making the only ripples as we paddled
into it. The dark mountains about it were seen through a glaucous
mist, and the brilliant white stems of the canoe-birches mingled
with the other woods around it. The wood-thrush sang on the distant
shore, and the laugh of some loons, sporting in a concealed western
bay, as if inspired by the morning, came distinct over the lake to us.*

—Henry David Thoreau, *The Maine Woods*

A long, sound sleep rejuvenated me, and I woke to the cheery
thought that today should be far simpler. Anticipating the evening's hot shower and Mama Bear's dinner, I quickly packed up. With
a large lake to cover, the earlier I got started, the better.

The meeting of Webster Brook with the East Branch is calm
and unremarkable. The latter comes bubbling down from the north,
where it gets its start less than ten miles away in a tiny pond surrounded by marsh. On second thought, however, perhaps this spot is
remarkable. Here, water from as far away as the Allagash Lake drainage arrives to feed the young and growing river.

Just a short way downstream sprawls 4,165-acre Grand Lake
Matagamon, half of it within the boundaries of Baxter State Park.
Before man intervened, there were two lakes here. In 1847, a tim-
ber crib dam was constructed at the southern end. A decade later,

Thoreau paddled through the swampy region between the lakes, along a winding, log-choked, somewhat elusive channel abounding in ducks. In the 1880s, the dam was rebuilt. The northwestern body of water, which I would reach first, is still known as Second Lake and the one to the southeast as First or Grand Lake.

To the Penobscot, Grand Lake and Second Lake were *Matangamook* and *Matangamooksis*. According to Kellogg, Matagamon comes from a Penobscot word meaning "the old, exhausted lake." Explaining further, he continues, "It has been said that hawks bred on the ledges of nearby Horse Mountain in such numbers that they depleted the population of partridges and ducks so that the Indians, on their hunts, found little or no food."

My first impression was rather gloomy. The East Branch ushered me into the marshy end of Second Lake, under bleak clouds. In the shallows, the skeleton of a deer glared up through the stagnant water, and I hurried on. As the lake widened, weak sun strove to part the clouds, and I felt my spirits lift. From here, it was only nine miles to the southern end. There, I would portage around the present-day dam back into the East Branch, just a half-mile above the Matagamon Wilderness campground.

Since the 1941 construction of a new and higher concrete dam, the lake attains depths of up to ninety-five feet. A more vital statistic, however, is the fact that a significant portion of the lake is only a few feet deep. Before long, I would be fervently wishing for just a few more inches of water.

Goose had hinted at challenges ahead, mysteriously titling this section of his trip report, "Grand Lake Matagamon: A land of mirages!" All too soon, I would know exactly what he'd meant.

On current maps, Grand Lake Matagamon appears as one continuous body of water. On paper, the connection between the two original lakes measures nearly a mile wide. Approaching this spot, however, Goose and Maverick had found the route they planned to take along the southern shore, between islands, impassable. As they tried to weave through, they ended up walking their canoe in two to four inches of water. At last, they discovered the channel "just north of a central path across Second Lake."

I hadn't been aware of the low lake levels until I read Maverick's trip report. By then, I was far from civilization without the opportunity to do any further research. A depth map of the lake, readily available online, would have been extremely helpful, but I hadn't thought to bring one.

Two hours after entering Second Lake, I was walking, too. *Slurping*, in fact, would be a much more descriptive word. I trudged along beside a dwindling ribbon of shallow stagnant water. In the muck and algae, frogs shot away in fright, leaving behind jets of silt. I tugged the boat forward, jerkily, a few feet at a time. My feet sank deep in the mud. Soon, they were caked with heavy gobs of the stuff. When one shoe eventually got sucked right off my foot, I yanked it out, then went on barefoot.

Where had my brilliant, island-studded lake gone?

When the boat would move no farther, I abandoned it and stubbornly went on. My mission—to find a route into the lower part of the lake. According to the map, I should have been surrounded by sparkling water, far from shore, and well past the spot that had slowed down my friends. Instead, turning back to gaze over my shoulder, I could see the yellow shape of my canoe waiting forlornly on a plain of sun-cracked brown. I wandered, past a rocky island marooned high and dry, then back north toward water glistening in the distance. I would have to retrace my steps, then make my way toward it.

How strange it seemed to be walking on the dry bed of the lake!

Occasionally, there were encouraging glimpses of water, which always turned out to be mere puddles. I washed my shoes off in one, then set them down to take a photo. Continuing back toward the boat, I suddenly remembered that I'd never picked up the shoes. Now this crazy woman was going back and forth frantically, from puddle to puddle, searching for dull, faded, mud-stained shoes in a sea of mud.

Thankfully, I found them.

How had I gotten in this predicament, especially when I'd been forewarned?

Once the sun shone, Second Lake had been alluring, fully living up to Thoreau's lyrical prose. In the softness of morning, the canoe glided forward without conscious thought, light and free.

Where a small point jutted out from the north shore, a pair of powerboats were visible against the dark-green shoreline. I was ready for company, after three days alone. I pointed the bow toward the sandy beach. As I drew closer, a man straightened up from tending the campfire and walked down, running his fingers through dark curly hair. He smiled and introduced himself, looking happy to have a visitor. We chatted for a while. Travis was a local who often came here from nearby Patten to camp with his family.

Afterward, I was impressed that they had navigated up as far as this campsite.

"We had to come see the lake," he explained. "I've never seen it this low. Wait till you get to the thoroughfare—it looks just like a salt marsh."

Crossing back to the south, I marveled at the abundance of bald eagles. Islands of dark, fractured rock rose steeply from the pale blue water, crowned with moss and clumps of pine. The eagles sought out the tallest trees, surveying the lake below from their regal perches.

At one island, I stole quietly along under the shelter of a bluff, until I was just beneath a mature eagle at the top of a tall red pine. His gaze rested far away. The softness of his feathers—white and chestnut brown—belied the power of his yellow hooked bill. When at last he flew, the beat of wings came like a rush from the sky above.

Four miles down Second Lake, the water shrank to just one narrow channel, but it seemed to be the right one. The landscape indeed resembled a salt marsh, where gulls roamed the green-tinged mud flats. Half an hour later, well past the narrows shown on the map, I turned south. Feeling victorious, I congratulated myself on having made it through the thoroughfare.

But where the waters of First Lake should have spread out before me, I found an ever-dwindling arm of water. At first, I could paddle and headed toward a line of trees in the distance, perhaps marking a channel. Double-checking the map, I could see that I should have

This was rapidly turning into a dead end

been surrounded by lake. Instead, after all that effort, I had to admit I was at a dead end. I returned to the canoe—luckily with my shoes—and retraced my steps until it would float once more.

The only open water lay to the north, and I followed. At first, it seemed I would turn up into a bay that led nowhere. *At least I'm moving*, I thought. Then, I found a way through—a channel close along the shore that led me to freedom at last. The good news was confirmed when I met a power boat motoring slowly toward me from the lower end of the lake. This is the way Travis and his family must have come.

Near a long island shaped like a comma, I stopped for a photo. On maps and in books, this place is alternately named Thoreau or Louse Island, inspired by two different points in history. On July 30, 1857, Thoreau and company stopped here and enjoyed a dinner of fried moose, from a cow that Polis had shot that day in the thoroughfare.

This island had also been one of the last stops for loggers emerging from winter camp.

"While on their spring drives," writes J. Parker Huber in *The Wildest Country: Exploring Thoreau's Maine*, "lumbermen performed a necessary task here. They kindled a fire, threw their winter clothes into the flames, and watched them turn to ash. They dubbed this place Louse Island, after the pest whose presence this ritual sought to eliminate."

In the foreground of my photo of the island, I proudly posed my smelly, rotten old river shoes up near the bow. They were decidedly my possession most in need of a roaring good bonfire.

A dense black cloud was taking shape behind Horse Mountain, ahead along the western shore. The profile of the mountain had a shape seen elsewhere in Maine, most notably on Moosehead Lake's Mount Kineo. A gently rising slope on the northern side and steep drop on the southern side can be attributed to the movement of glacial ice long ago. Thoreau, too, had made this observation.

The storm might move away, but then again it might not, I mused. Consequently, I decided to take a lunch break at a boat landing in a small cove. I would rest and see what the storm did. At the end of a long pier, a couple of teenagers lazily dangled fishing poles, and on the shoreline road, vehicles slowed as they approached the northern entrance to Baxter State Park.

I unpacked my lunch at a picnic table under a small pavilion. When it began to sprinkle, I sprinted down to flip the canoe and hustle back with my bags. Content, I gazed out at the growing downpour from my dry retreat. Not only was I comfortable, but the dam at the south end of the lake was only a mile or so away, so there was no need to rush. When the rain ended, I would put back in.

However, there was one more stop I hoped to make.

"The place is hard to miss, and the view is spectacular. The beach curves around, looking out across the lake toward the mountains. It's a cabin, and the logs are a weathered red now. It once belonged to the writer Edmund Ware Smith and his wife, Mary, you know, before Jake."

I hadn't known that, but now felt even more compelled to visit the place.

My friend Sandi Day and I were chatting in downtown Damariscotta, the coastal community that's been home for me since I moved to Maine. It was June, and preparations for my trip were in full swing. I wanted to know how to find her family's camp on Grand Lake Matagamon, so I could stop by for a visit. She wasn't sure if she would be there, but its history intrigued me, and I wanted to take a peek.

Sandi's eyes lit up with enthusiasm when I asked about the camp.

"I sure would love to paddle with you," she volunteered, and I knew she meant every word.

Under dark-blond curls, eyes crinkling with laughter, Sandi's compact form exudes energy. She is always busy, always juggling multiple projects, and she's good at it. Today, Sandi was selling little yellow rubber ducks, to be raced down the Damariscotta River and under the town bridge, as a fundraiser for one of our local conservation organizations, whose board she led.

As I picked out some ducks with lucky numbers, she gave me directions. Unfortunately, we did not have a map. Wishing for one, I tried to picture the lake and place the camp in its correct location.

Sandi's husband Dan is the grandson of artist Maurice "Jake" Day, a Damariscotta native born there in 1892. Initially, I had discovered Jake's work through a heart-warming local holiday tradition. It all began during World War II, when Jake was looking to take his mind off the worry of having sons serving in the military. He began creating lighted dioramas of moonlit winter landscapes, snowy villages and Christmas scenes, some incorporating the whimsical animal characters that were his trademark. Woodland creatures sang carols, fairy tales came to life, and the stable animals gathered around the manger to await the birth of baby Jesus. Each December, the collection of dioramas is displayed downtown on chilly winter nights.

Jake is probably best known for the role he played in shaping the characters and setting of the much-loved 1942 Disney movie *Bambi*. A 1915 graduate of the school of the Boston Museum of Fine Arts, Jake became a book and magazine illustrator, editorial cartoonist, wood carver, and talented watercolor painter. In 1936, he and his wife Bea, with sons McClure and Richard, drove across the country to California. The paintings he brought along secured him a job with the MGM Studio. When MGM loaned him to the Disney Studio to work on *Bambi*, Jake convinced Walt Disney that the movie's main character should be a white-tailed deer. As a result, many of the movie's scenes, as well as its animals and plants, were inspired by the woodlands of Baxter State Park.

To the writer fall many solemn and sacred responsibilities. The moment when one embraces the task of writing about a place, one becomes part of its enduring chronicle, a thought at once humbling and empowering. Keen observation, the ability to translate its spirit into the written word, and a reverence for the past are all required. The experience becomes all the richer when one comes to know those who have gone before, at times solely through the art and writing they have left behind.

No better example comes to mind than the trio of Jake Day, his closest friend, Lester Hall, and writer Edmund Ware Smith, whose relationships with the Katahdin region are forever united. All came to love this wild country with an intimacy and passion born of countless days spent there. Lester was the first to come, with friends in the summer of 1928, driving an old Essex until the road ran out and their explorations continued afoot.

In 1933, Jake first accepted Lester's invitation to visit the area. Over the next twenty-five years, they would make at least sixteen additional expeditions together, visiting in all seasons. In fact, according to *Katahdin Comrades: The Journals of Lester F. Hall*, edited by Hall's daughter Charlotte Hall Kirkpatrick, the pair got their first look at the present-day national monument on snowshoes, in March 1935. Guided by friend Caleb Scribner and accompanied by Jake's son Mac, Dan's father, they descended the west bank of the river beyond Bowlin Falls. The "wild fury of the spring break-up" had just begun. Seeing the legendary falls and pitches, Lester wrote, "one could not but marvel at the intrepid spirit of the men who with the crude basic tools of that time forced this wild river to do their bidding."

After moving to California, Jake missed a few years of these outings. Imagine the friends' delight, then, when an offer came from Disney in 1938 to spend a month in the Katahdin region, all expenses paid. The expedition had dual objectives, according to Dan and Sandi Day.

"First, Walt wanted real woodland animals for his artists to draw. With the help and blessings of the Maine Warden and Fish and Game Services, Jake sent two orphaned deer, named Bambi and Faline, and some rabbits and skunks, by train to the Disney Studio in Burbank, California, as models for the artists. Next, Walt wanted Jake to photograph and sketch the flora as backdrops for the movie."

Jake brought along the *Bambi* script, and long days were spent rambling the mountain trails, peat bogs, and wild ravines where clear streams cascaded into mossy pools, like the one they christened "Diana's Bath." Jake took endless photographs and gathered samples of woodland plants, carefully packed them in damp moss, and mailed them off to the studio.

"We are on the watch constantly for a place which presumably could be the birthplace of Bambi and the glade or meadow in which the woods characters assembled for food and play," Lester explained.

After weeks of searching, in a meadow along Wassataquoik Stream, they found the perfect spot.

"This is Bambi's birthplace," they thought. "Here is the clearing where the forest creatures came for food and play. Here is the edge of the forest where they disappeared when danger threatened. And here is the little knoll from which the elder deer could keep an eye on their offspring."

By 1940, even before *Bambi* was released, Jake was homesick for Maine and brought his family home to his 1798 homestead in Damariscotta. There, he reconnected with old friends and made some prestigious new ones. By the '50s, Jake had been appointed "Colonel" of a group of Damariscotta-area sportsmen who called themselves "Jake's Rangers." Among them were a postmaster, a veterinary surgeon, a grocery store owner, a physician, and an "insurance man." In 1959, Lester was made an Honorary Colonel, although he never again went north before he died in 1962.

Sandi had given me quick directions to the camp, but I was relying on memory, as I hadn't been able to write anything down at the time. There was a chance that Sandi would be there, hoping for a visit. I had expected to find the camp close to the dam or at least visible from it. As I neared the south end of the lake, I looked back. Standing high and proud on the east shore was a camp, in clear view, though quite a distance away. I was surprised that I hadn't noticed it earlier. That had to be the place.

After backtracking roughly two miles, I landed on a sandy beach and walked up to investigate. Clumps of birch trees along the shore obscured the view to the west, explaining why I hadn't noticed the house earlier. Now that I was here, I could see this was not the right place. The house was too new, with shingles instead of weathered red logs. The name alone almost made it worth the trip, however. CAMP WINDL BLOW was the perfect moniker for a camp on a large northern lake!

The hunt for Jake's cabin would have to wait until tomorrow.

Portaging into the East Branch was simple. Above the dam on the right, I took out at the Matagamon Wilderness boat landing, carried down the road past the dam keeper's house, and put back in down a steep path. In a few minutes, I was at the campground and the same familiar site I'd had last time.

"Don't you ever just cry?"

Sue Christianson, her daughter Katie, and daughter-in-law Brandi were thankful I had arrived in one piece. As I recounted some of the high and low points, they asked lots of questions, amazed at some of what I'd been through. I guess I had come close to crying a few times. When the never-ending ledge drops above Roll Dam caught me out as darkness fell on my first night. Pushing upstream on Caucomgomoc Stream, convinced that I was doing something absolutely insane. And just the day before, in the stretch between Indian Carry and Grand Pitch, now just a foggy blur in my memory.

All that was behind me now. I happily dug into a bacon, mushroom, and black olive pizza, washed down with ginger ale. With my dessert of tea and cookies, I sorted through email and wrote to my family, then promised to come back early the next morning for breakfast.

Camped next to me was a large group from Wavus, which is Kieve's sister camp on Damariscotta Lake. The girls were also running the East Branch, ending at Medway, about nine miles farther than I was going. When I woke early the next morning, I was just in time to see them go. There had been another loud thunderstorm in the night, with more rain to help our river levels. The girls turned to wave, helmets on every head. *I wish I could see them run Stair Falls*, I thought. They paddled matching green canoes, the rest a colorful medley of youthful exuberance and courage.

Joe Christianson was cooking that morning. While I ate fluffy blueberry pancakes and bacon, with a giant glass of orange juice, he came out to the dining room to visit. I asked him about water levels, and recounted my trials getting through to First Lake.

"The dam is releasing about 450 to 500 cubic feet per second," he answered. "In a normal summer, it's about 250. They started work on the bridge, and it was worse than they thought."

I didn't understand, at first, why additional repairs to the road bridge in view out the window would mean more water coming through now to help my trip. Joe elaborated. The lake was being brought down a total of five feet now, to be able to contain more rainwater and release less volume when the bridge work resumed. Later in the summer, they would drop the lake level another five or six feet to work on the dam, repairing the concrete and installing steel plating to limit ice damage.

I wondered if boats would still be able to get through from First to Second Lake when the lake was even lower. Joe assured me that they would, then brought me a map.

"I don't know why I didn't think to give you this when you were here last time," he apologized. He showed me where he'd marked the channel in pink highlighter. This was the course of the original stream connecting the two lakes, the route that had finally brought me safely through the previous day.

"You don't know where Jake Day's camp is, do you? I'm friends with Sandi Day, whose husband is Jake's grandson. She invited me to stop by, but I couldn't find it yesterday."

"Jake used to work for Disney," he remembered. Back he went toward the kitchen to get his DeLorme Atlas. He showed me where the camp was, about five or six miles up the east shore.

"You don't need to paddle all the way out there. You can take my truck. The keys are in it, right out there by the sign. There's no hurry. I'm not going anywhere."

This quick northwoods generosity still takes me by surprise. I thanked Joe profusely, then drove off, carefully following his directions. From the main road, I turned left onto the dirt and gravel of the Boy Scout Road. Hand-painted mile markers tracked my progress. I was passing through Penobscot Indian Nation territory, and then, on a faded sign, I could just make out the words, "Jake's Rangers," urging me on. Not far past Mile 5, I turned into Jake's driveway and reverently climbed out.

Sadly, there was no other vehicle around. Evidently, no one was home.

Without a doubt, however, this was the place. It was a rustic camp, with character and a glorious view of the lake and mountains, befitting Jake's Rangers, and the man whom I would come to know through his writing as plain old Ed Smith. There hadn't been time before the trip to pick up any of Ed's books. That would come later, but it would be worth the wait.

The Day family camp, originally built by Ed and Mary Smith from logs cut on their property

The cabin looked as if it had been built in stages, with no thought-out plan. Part of one side had been repainted dark brown, but vestiges of the original barn red paint clung to the rest of the rough logs. Peeking inside, I saw wood-paneled comfort and a huge round spool table painted red, with stools to match. Here the gang no doubt gathered to plot their next adventure and tell tall tales about the last. A solid desk, vintage photos, old rugs, and a mission style chair with green cushions beckoned.

As I gazed through the dusty glass, how I wished I could pull one of those stools up to the table, rest my elbows, prop my chin, and listen in. *The stories this place could tell.*

Luckily for me, Ed had captured some of the more colorful capers. Jake first met Ed in 1954, when he was commissioned to provide drawings for some of his magazine articles. The following summer, Jake and Lester boated over for lunch with Ed and Mary, in this very cabin, which the couple had built a decade earlier. In their first summers on the lake, supplies came in by boat and mail by plane. By 1955, they were ready to live in Maine year-round and bought a winter home near Damariscotta.

Ed wrote for a host of magazines, including *Outdoor Life*, *Better Homes and Gardens*, *Field and Stream*, *The Saturday Evening Post*, and *Sports Illustrated*. Some of his most popular articles and books chronicle the ongoing battle between his fictional One-Eyed Poacher, Jeff Coongate, and the local game warden, but Ed Smith had another, deeper side. He had come from the city and wrote vividly of the awe and wonder of coming to belong to this place that is the Maine north woods. Here were stories to take along in the canoe, to savor one tale at a time by the light of a lantern.

One evening by the woodstove, long after I had returned home, I was drawn in by Smith's delightful book, *A Treasury of the Maine Woods*. Ed's soul was in his words, in his stories of family, mortality, and the lakes he knew as friends. Here was the wilderness where I, too, was at home. There was incomprehensible loss in "The Magic Woodsman," the glow and gravity of a fish fry with Eisenhower in "Mr. Smith Meets the President," and even an ode to the loon. The cover illustration and inside sketches came from the brushes and pen of Jake Day.

Jake's Rangers camped at Russell Pond in Baxter State Park, from left: Dr. McClure "Mac" Day (veterinary surgeon), Edward Pierce (grocery store owner), Edmund Ware Smith (author), Bentley Glidden (postmaster), Maurice "Jake" Day (artist), Jack Glidden (insurance agent), and Dr. Sam Belknap (physician)

As the years went by, Ed wrote about, and no doubt embellished, the exploits of Jake's Rangers, becoming an honorary member of the group. It was this public notoriety that led to another distinguished visit, this time from Supreme Court Justice William O. Douglas. The story of how that turned into a long, rewarding friendship is found within the pages of *Upriver & Down: Stories from the Maine Woods*. Justice Douglas, an enthusiastic participant in many an adventure, was also eventually named an honorary Jake's Ranger.

The dedication of *Upriver & Down* reads, "This book is for that lean, talented, moccasin-shod, woods-roaming artist and photographer of Damariscotta, Maine—by name, Maurice Day; by nickname, 'Jake'; and by authority of 'Jake's Rangers,' 'The Colonel.' Affectionately, E.W.S."

CHAPTER 13

THE GIFT OF A RIVER

The face of the river, in time, became a wonderful book...which told its mind to me without reserve, delivering its most cherished secrets as clearly as if it had uttered them with a voice. And it was not a book to be read once and thrown aside, for it had a new story to tell every day.

—**Mark Twain,** *Life on the Mississippi*

Once upon a time, not long after the days of flowered vans and peace signs, a young artist married. In the spirit of *The Good Life* embraced by Helen and Scott Nearing, she and her husband built a cabin in rural Maine, off the grid. Although their marriage didn't last, the woman stayed there to raise her children in a home with no running water or electricity.

That young mother, Roxanne Quimby, was committed heart and soul to taking from the world no more than she contributed. To treading lightly on all that nature had bestowed. She had her twins, Hannah and Lucas, and was living life on her own terms. Life, however, has a way of delivering us into uncharted waters, at times far from our intended destination.

One day, Quimby met a neighbor, Burt Shavitz, a beekeeper who sold honey from the back of his pickup. In time, the pair became partners in business and in life. Traveling to craft fairs, they sold honey, now in pretty little jars, and handmade beeswax candles. Their home business grew exponentially, as Quimby blossomed as an entrepreneur. She continually developed and tested new offerings, from furniture polish and floor wax to soaps and pet products, but it was her all-natural, earth-friendly beeswax lip balm that would ultimately become the catalyst for a new level of financial success.

The enterprise flourished, adding employees, offices, and a name now recognized worldwide: Burt's Bees. Yes, the face that adorned millions of those beeswax-yellow tubes of lotion and lip balm was that of a man who was always most comfortable selling honey in gallon jars by the side of the road.

In another time, I was a farmer's wife, peddling homegrown sweet corn, tomatoes, and butter beans in the thick summer heat, along a country road. I've risen at dawn to arrange colorful bushels of freshly harvested produce in the bed of a truck. Greeted favorite customers week after week, weighing their orders on an old-fashioned scale, with a small child helping. It's an honest, fulfilling way of life. Did Quimby, I wonder, take stock one day and realize her chosen lifestyle was but a distant memory?

By 1995, the company had relocated to business-friendly North Carolina, leaving behind its Maine roots. In 1999, Quimby bought out Shavitz's one-third share of the company. In 2003, with annual sales approaching $60 million, Quimby sold an 80-percent interest in Burt's Bees to AEA Investors. When the Clorox Company purchased AEA in 2007, Quimby sold her remaining holdings, bringing her total proceeds to an estimated $300 million or more.

Ironically, through the uncaring vehicle of capitalism, Quimby now stood poised to return full circle to the ideals of her youth—to give more than she took, and to give that gift to the people of Maine and the nation. With generosity reminiscent of Percival P. Baxter, Quimby purchased tens of thousands of acres of Maine's northern forest, then offered to donate the land for a national park.

Like Baxter's stance on water rights, however, some of Quimby's decisions flamed the fires of opposition to the project. I thought back to the signs that still screamed, "NATIONAL PARK NO," so vehemently on the drive into the monument. Initially, Quimby banned many traditional uses of her land, including hunting, trapping, snowmobiling, and four-wheeling. For those with cabins there, the consequences were far more devastating. Quimby did not renew the leases that some families had held for decades. She gave them a year to move their cabins, or they would be demolished.

In Maine, widespread access to both public and private land provides the foundation of a lifestyle that we often take for granted. What we view as a right is, in truth, a privilege. When that lifestyle is compromised, feelings run strong. Change is always difficult, and Mainers were much more accustomed to state, not federal, ownership of public lands.

In the fall of 2011, the tenor of the conversation began to change when Quimby's son, Lucas St. Clair, took over the leadership of Elliotsville Plantation Inc. (EPI), the Quimby family foundation that owned and managed the land. St. Clair is energetic, personable, and positive, an outdoorsman who even coauthored, with his wife, a book entitled the *AMC Guide to Winter Hiking and Camping*.

As President of EPI, St. Clair took a much different, more collaborative approach. In effect, he began the listening process that has become the starting point for creating the National Park Service's future management plan for Katahdin Woods and Waters. At lunch one day, I asked him how that worked.

In his words, St. Clair remembers saying, "Look, there is no proposal. So, let's figure that out collectively, as a community, as a state, as the Park Service. Let's figure out what we can and can't do and try to create something that is going to work for as many people as possible."

St. Clair went out and literally had thousands of conversations with individuals. Of course, there was never any question that EPI would pursue federal protection of the land in some form, whether as a national park or a national monument. Given that fact, he asked people what would satisfy them.

"So, we heard from loads of people about snowmobiling and hunting and fishing and ATVs and wilderness and bird watching and backcountry areas and hiking and paddling and camping and RVs, just the whole gambit. We were able to take a lot of that input and craft something that is going to work for a wide variety of people. That's what it took, that and time."

Those in favor of a national park dreamed of increased tourism dollars, higher real estate values, and businesses relocating to a region that had been economically depressed by the closure of the paper mills that had been its backbone. To them, this place was a natural treasure, rich in history and scenic beauty, that would be preserved for generations to come.

Although a new, more unified energy began to surround the idea of establishing a national park, there was still bitter opposition. Those against the idea argued all over the board. Some thought there was nothing to see there but cutover land and dusty logging roads that wouldn't attract many visitors. Others argued that increased visitation would forever change this place they loved, citing noise, security concerns, and negative environmental impacts.

Since the moment he took office in 2011, Maine Governor Paul LePage had strongly opposed the idea of a national park. In April 2016, a bill opposing the establishment of the proposed national monument narrowly passed both the Maine House and Senate. The state, however, had no real power to prevent the creation of the national monument, which would happen by presidential proclamation under the authority of the Antiquities Act of 1906.

So, at last, in August 2016, Katahdin Woods and Waters National Monument became a reality.

The following month, the National Park Service held four public listening sessions in the region, inviting community input into future monument planning. To ensure a fair and efficient process, a neutral facilitator, Leigh Tillman, organized and ran the meetings. Her resulting 144-page report documents every response shared at the sessions or during the written comment period. In total, more than 550 people attended, and over 75 wrote in, providing a comprehensive summary of opinions within local communities, the state, and beyond.

Many of the same hopes were expressed by a wide range of attendees. Local schools would have their own outdoor place to learn. Young families would come home to stay. Portions of the park would be accessible for those with mobility issues. The heritage of the Wabanaki and the raw story of the logging days would be brought to life. Maine's Baxter State Park and the federally owned monument would be collaborative partners, complementing one another. Rare species, dark skies, wildlife corridors, heritage trout ponds, and traditional land uses like fiddlehead foraging would all be preserved.

It was a tall order. Monument planners would strive to achieve a

balance that fulfilled these dreams, while addressing the concerns and
sometimes conflicting desires of a broad array of stakeholders.

Almost two years later, this ambitious undertaking was well un-
derway, and there was progress to be seen, in the woods and on the
waters. I had experienced the monument from one perspective, driving in on the Loop Road with map in hand, then following historic
trails through the ancient Appalachians. Now, it was time to embark
upon the river that flowed through the heart of the monument. The
days ahead, the last of my journey, would test my whitewater skills
and bring to light the ecological diversity, human experience, flora
and fauna of this wild waterway. I couldn't wait.

To navigate, I had just purchased an additional resource. The
brand-new waterproof Katahdin Woods and Waters trail map, with
topo lines, was a project of the Friends of Katahdin Woods and Waters
and published by Map Adventures. With Zip Kellogg's Delorme
booklet, the Thoreau–Wabanaki Trail map of the East Branch, and
the AMC river guide, I would have plenty of references.

I carefully parked Joe's pickup back where I'd found it, thanked him
once more, and said farewell.

The sun shone strong on my shoulders as I committed myself to
the river, the current quickly embracing the boat. The tranquility of the
first few miles gave no hint of what awaited me downstream. Birches
leaned out over rippling water, and an osprey soared high above.

In the slow current, I overtook a young boy drifting lazily along
in a plump inner tube. Soon, I could see the rest of his group—two
grandparents enjoying some summer fun with their grandchildren.
One teenage girl stretched out on a plump pink pool float, while the
rest were in an assortment of tubes.

From time to time, the current quickened, and there were rocks
to avoid. I stopped to check out the amenities at the first campsite,
Upper East Branch, about two miles along on river right. It was well-
marked, on a straight stretch with a small island in view ahead. Stone
steps led up to a large, flat clearing big enough to accommodate a
group, with two picnic tables, a fire pit, and a privy.

Thoreau had camped a mile or more downriver on the night of July 30, 1857, just a day later in the summer than I was passing by. It was fun to think that he had experienced the river in much the same season. There was no sign marking the spot that he christened "Checkerberry-Tea Camp," in honor of the new flavor of tea that Joe Polis prepared that evening.

Thoreau's checkerberry (*Gaultheria procumbens*) is a low-growing evergreen plant with glossy dark-green leaves. Its drooping white flowers of July turn to bright-red berries in the fall. I know the same plant as wintergreen. In 1999, wintergreen was designated Maine's official state herb.

Its medicinal properties and pleasant flavor make wintergreen a good choice for tea. The Penobscot used the crushed leaves to relieve sore muscles and inflammation. Brewed as tea, it calmed upset stomachs and eased sore throats. During the Revolutionary War, colonists turned to wintergreen as a replacement for the heavily taxed imported British tea.

Soon I had the first of many views of the mountains that accompany the East Branch paddler. Traveler Mountain is often visible in this upper section. The highest point in the monument is on its slopes, at an elevation of 2,350 feet. Its summit, at 3,541 feet, lies just within the boundaries of Baxter State Park, due west of Haskell Rock Pitch. The peak, much higher than any within the monument, is so named because it seems to travel along as you descend the river.

The river began to twist and turn, doubling back on itself through a section called The Oxbow. I paddled down a wide shallow avenue overhung with silver maples and dotted with white Queen Anne's lace and the brilliant red spikes of the cardinal flower. There was an air of sleepy peace here, and an openness in the light sunny grasses of the riverbanks.

A large backwater on the left, almost a pond, invited exploration. I spent a while "gunkholing," as Dad would have called it, winding my way silently into hidden places, with no particular purpose. From deep in the marsh came the strident honking of a family of Canada geese, and the air hummed with insect life. In barely half an hour, I observed three noteworthy plant species, hinting at the ecological diversity waiting to be discovered.

The first was arrowhead, whose three-petaled white flowers with yellow centers stood out in clumps on tall bright-green stems. This plant, named for the shape of its leaf, produces edible root tubers that were a valuable Native American food source. High in starch and phosphorous, the tubers can be cooked many ways, ground into flour, or even candied with maple sugar. Certain tribes used arrowhead to treat headaches, indigestion, and tuberculosis.

Penetrating further into the shallows, the submerged vegetation became almost too thick to push through. Much of the dense tangled mat was composed of the runners and delicate, branching fan-shaped leaves of white water crowfoot, a native aquatic perennial. Its five-petaled white flowers, also with yellow centers, floated on the surface, and clusters of little round green fruits were visible on underwater stems.

The third plant was new to me, and I did not identify it until much later. This native wetland species, called several-veined sweetflag (*Acorus americanus*), has a distinctive appearance. Its lance-shaped leaves are stiff and thick, about one-half-inch wide and several feet tall, with a prominent raised vein running the length of the leaf. Later I learned that the leaves are sweetly fragrant if crushed. What caught my eye were the two-inch-long green flower heads that protruded at an angle directly from the stems.

According to the Native Plant Trust, "Native American use of several-veined sweetflag probably played a role in determining its distribution, as the plant was highly prized for its medicinal properties, widely traded, and wild-planted along trade routes. Disjunct populations now occur at sites that are close to old Native American villages. The rhizome contains the medicinal properties and is used to treat a variety of conditions from nausea, heartburn, and colds to fatigue and anxiety."

I maneuvered the boat around, further flustering the geese, and retreated, back the way I'd come.

The Oxbow is bracketed by two unimproved campsites, Oxbow East at the start and Stair Falls East at the end, both on river left. Though lacking tables or privies, they did have fire pits. The latter, around four and a half miles from Matagamon Wilderness, particularly appealed to me.

I found the campsite just around a bend crowned with a halo of pink Joe Pye weed beneath a perfect blue-and-white sky. I climbed up to explore. A cooling breeze blew through the high site, and I could see a couple of potential tent spots among the rocks. Looking back downstream, sun-dappled mountains rose above a marshy shoreline that looked ideal for evening wildlife viewing. This was my favorite of the three sites I'd passed so far.

My anticipation grew as I left The Oxbow behind. I was ready for some action. My palms tightened on the paddle at the unmistakable sound of whitewater ahead. "Two straightforward Class II rapids" preceded Stair Falls, according to the Thoreau–Wabanaki Trail map. The second was "best approached on river left." I ran both without incident, finding them a good warm-up for things to come.

Then, there I was, at the campsite where I'd first met Goose and Maverick during my backpacking trip, eighteen days earlier. Stair Falls is rated Class II+ to light Class III, and I clearly remembered how easy they'd made it look. Goose had proclaimed the water level "perfect for their travels." "Smitten" by the rapids of the East Branch, they found all the drops without mandatory portages very runnable. Stair Falls was the first, where they "happily ran the gently traversing line from right of center gradually toward river right where the ledges had clear tongues to run down." My goal was to run it also, assisted by slightly higher water flows than they had experienced.

However, I walked the length of the two-tenths-of-a-mile portage trail and just couldn't make up my mind. I was alone with a Kevlar canoe, and the carry to bypass it would be a piece of cake. From the best vantage point I could find along shore, I gazed upstream, mentally tracing route after route down the perfectly shaped staircase. I ate lunch and continued to ponder what to do.

An hour later, my canoe rested safely below the rapid. I pulled out my journal and wrote:

Just 443 steps down the portage trail. I chose not to run Stair Falls. I hope that doesn't make me less of a person. I feel like less of a person.

Happily, there was no time to mope. The mid-afternoon sun reminded me that it was time to move along, that there were other challenges ahead. The Haskell Deadwater would have been another great spot to explore, but within twenty minutes, I was through its quiet waters and pulling out for the portage around Haskell Rock Pitch. There was the Haskell Deadwater campsite that I'd visited on my hike, and another uncomplicated portage trail, about a third of a mile long.

As I carried along it, refreshing currents of misty air wafted up from falls, discernibly cooler. Haskell Rock still looked just as strange. It was nearing five o'clock when I finished repacking the boat, carefully securing every item. Below Haskell Rock Pitch were three rapids that would give me a chance to redeem myself. Kellogg calls them Class II+. The Thoreau–Wabanaki Trail map gives two of them names, which we know is never a good thing. Micilic I and Micilic II. Perhaps they were named for another unfortunate riverman.

I got in trouble midway through the first one, when an unseen ledge cut off any possibility of making it through unscathed. I hung there, then worked my way off, and ended up running backwards down the last part. I walked the second, then redeemed myself by running the third perfectly. It was nice to end the day on a note of victory!

A quarter mile past the last rapid, I rounded a sharp bend and spotted the start of the Pond Pitch portage trail on river right. Both banks have portage trails, but it was the Pond Pitch West Campsite that had so appealed to me when I'd backpacked through, so I stuck to the west shore.

By early evening, the idyllic spot was all mine, with a tidy camp all set up. Serenity and contentment flooded through me, born of this place and of all that the day had brought. Not to mention my forethought in packing a bottle of Samuel Adams Summer Ale and a bag of Fritos Flavor Twists. Life was good.

CHAPTER 14

MONUMENTAL TREASURES

A gentle, gradual fading of light, the sun's afterglow, tints the high clouds. Reds pale to pink, then pearl. Sharp shadows lose their character, meld and melt. Long-held moments of the visible become memories. Evening: to make even, to bring to balance, to restore equanimity. Often, stillness settles on the summer air at nightfall. A slight breeze and coolness pass over the grasses and the breathing leaves. A peaceful sense of settling down, a slow closing of the eye of day, first a drowsy blink, then another follows. Watchful stars emerge, taking charge after evening has given her quiet sigh.

—**Ted Clapp,** *Tell Me About the River*

Isat by the falls, cradling a warm pot of potato bacon soup and trying with finely crafted words to do justice to the scene before me. *Pond Pitch descends ten feet, the falling itself a work of art. A curving arc of roughhewn rock spans the river, creating a myriad of paths for the water to follow. In places, the flow is silky and smooth as honey. In others, it is as if there are a hundred tiny waterfalls issuing forth from solid rock. These grow, surging into fountains of white-churned foam. The heart of the pitch is simply boiling white that drops in stages, gathering up the silky waters and the tiny cascades to fill the gorge, below a craggy shoreline on which bold spruce and their brothers reach toward heaven. Wild, untamed, relentless, a primal power that will endure, long after we have gone our way.*

Later, beside the fading glow of a campfire, I cheered the stars as they blinked on, seeming as close as I had ever seen them. The vivid moon hung there, just past full. I wonder if, in that moment, I quite appreciated what I was seeing. The skies above the monument are among the darkest in the eastern United States. This is not just a flowery statement but based on clear data. According to the Maine IAT, the monument's sky quality meter reading is "on a par with the remote sites selected for world-class observatories."

Only one out of three people on Earth can see the Milky Way from where they live.

The Bortle Scale rates nighttime skies on a scale of 1 (Antarctica) to 9 (Inner-city). The skies above me were a 2, defined by the scale's creator John Bortle as a "truly dark site" where "the summer Milky Way is highly structured to the unaided eye, and its brightest parts look like veined marble when viewed with ordinary binoculars."

From my innermost being, I wanted this part of the monument experience to be protected. For something on Earth to remain unchanged, so that in a hundred years, another soul might look upward from this riverbank and ponder the universe. Luckily, there is a process for doing just that.

The International Dark-Sky Association (IDA) reports that light pollution worldwide is growing at a rate of 2 percent per year. The continual increase in outdoor lighting negatively impacts human health, carbon emissions, and wildlife behavior. Birds migrate too early or late or wander from their migration routes. Nocturnal hunters and prey alike now live in a much brighter nighttime world. Insects drawn to electric lights die, and entire ecosystems are deprived of food and pollinators.

Through education and outreach, public policy development and certification of dark-sky-friendly lighting fixtures, IDA strives to preserve dark skies for future generations. In 2001, IDA created the International Dark Sky Places Program, which the national monument aspires to join. Working together, the National Park Service, Elliotsville Foundation Inc. (the successor to EPI), and the Friends of Katahdin Woods and Waters have applied for designation of the monument as an International Dark Sky Sanctuary. A sanctuary is one of six designations within the program, defined as one of the "most remote (and often darkest) places in the world whose conservation state is most fragile." For the monument, that fragility may stem from how easily current conditions could change.

Lucas St. Clair is optimistic that the monument will achieve this designation. During the application process, he recalled, "One thing they asked was how many incandescent light bulbs there were, and we counted, and there were nine."

IDA responded by saying, "What? You actually physically have to go and count every light bulb."

"We did and there are nine," was St. Clair's confident reply.

That simple statement, and the fact that the monument is adjacent to places like Baxter State Park—which uses no electricity except at its entrance gates—helps explain why it deserves to become a sanctuary. If accepted, future efforts would include working with surrounding communities to remain dark-sky friendly, as infrastructure is added to support increased visitation.

In general, dark-sky friendly outdoor lighting is shielded, downward facing, and tailored to what is needed for safety and security. As the popularity of energy efficient LED lighting grows, it is important to understand the range of Kelvin light temperatures available. Counterintuitive to what you might guess, LEDs with cooler light temperatures of 3000K or less have a pleasing red or yellow hue, while also better protecting night skies. Bulbs with hotter light temperatures of more than 3000K to 5000K emit a harsher, blue-hued light that is more damaging to night skies.

Interestingly, natural sunlight has a light temperature of around 5000K, the same as the least desirable LED lighting. This fact makes it easy to understand why the bluer LEDs can so disrupt the circadian rhythms of plants and animals alike, making them believe that night has become day.

By seven in the morning, the stars had faded, and the sun emerged after a chilly night. An hour later, I had paddled a half-mile downstream and was preparing to carry around Grand Pitch on river left. Although both shores have portage trails, I wanted to explore the east shore this time. I lifted my boat out at a small beach, just before the river made a bend to the left.

The portage trail passed through two unimproved campsites. The first was a spacious site with a fire pit, just above the takeout, and the second a small site much nearer the waterfall. Fresh and well rested, I breezed through the one-third-mile carry in fifteen minutes, even getting a good look at a garter snake from my limited under-canoe vantage point.

"Grand Pitch on the East Branch is something to behold," Goose had declared.

I agreed, thinking that the best perspective was from this angle in the soft light of morning. The effect was glorious. I picked handfuls of ripe blueberries from the bushes all around, then sank down on a cushion of moss to take in the scene before me. From upriver, strong arms of sunlit forest guided the brisk waters around boulders and craggy ledges toward the drop. At the brink, the river tumbled with abandon into churning white. Here and there, within the falls, pockets of greenish water held steady and true. Like the flicker of flames,

Its twenty-foot drop makes Grand Pitch the highest waterfall in the monument

the never-ending movement was mesmerizing, holding me rapt for long minutes. At last, with a fond farewell, I stood up to go.

The last of the four rapids with mandatory portages lay a half-mile ahead. I admired its unique and creative name—the Hulling Machine. Grand Pitches seemed to be in plentiful supply, with three in the nearby environs, on Webster Stream, the East Branch, and the Seboeis River.

I felt sure that there were no other Hulling Machines!

This rapid, writes Kellogg, was "so named in log driving days because it removed bark from the logs being driven down the river. It's easy to see how it might have ripped the bark from a log. What's hard to imagine is that there was anything left of a log after it was tossed like a matchstick through these frothing falls. This descent must have approximated an automatic wood pulping process."

The short stretch of river between Grand Pitch and the Hulling Machine was quick and fun, with friendly rapids. I found the start of the half-mile portage just before the river bent to the right, thus obscuring any good view of the turmoil below. This was the most difficult of the East Branch carries. I added my footprints to the squishy mud, balanced gingerly on rocks, and kept my footing where the trail grew steep and slippery. At one point, the path seemed about to turn away from the river. I hesitated but trusted that I should keep on going. I was rewarded when the trail returned eventually to the river shore, where I had lunch and filtered some more water. So far, it had taken me three hours to go 1.7 miles.

Although the four mandatory portages were behind me, I wasn't quite finished with whitewater for the day. A mile ahead lay Bowlin Falls, a short Class II–III drop, possibly runnable. Just after passing between a pair of rocky bluffs, I found the start of the portage at a pool on river right. I walked the two-tenth-mile-long trail, not finding much to indicate the campsite shown only on the Thoreau–Wabanaki Trail map. This drop looked like another tricky one, extending most of the way across the river from the left bank. Again, I wavered and imagined myself dumping, with no one to help.

In my journal that evening, I wrote that I probably could and should have run Bowlin Falls, but I did not. Now, reflecting on that decision, and others like it, I stand firm in the belief that you should trust your instincts in the moment. Don't chastise yourself for being conservative, especially when you're out there alone.

That day, it also cheered me a bit to know that more challenges awaited downriver. Whetstone Falls and Crowfoot Rapids would give me two more opportunities to prove my mettle.

An abundance of effort had brought me ten miles so far, from Matagamon Wilderness to Bowlin Falls. The next ten miles promised to be more relaxed. The river would descend only eighty feet in this distance, compared to more than two hundred feet in the first stretch.

I would need to find a campsite for the night, but there were several options and little competition. My only companions on the river seemed to be the Wavus girls. Back on the water, I rounded a bend and saw their canoes pulled up in an even row on the shore below Bowlin Camps. Strong strokes carried me past, under the bridge that I'd crossed while backpacking, and onward into new territory.

The Spring Brook campsite, a mile ahead on river right, came quickly and much too soon for my evening camp. I whisked through lively, entertaining Class I Spencer Rips, which brought back pleasant memories of running Allagash Rips in years past. After that, I found only intermittent quickwater or tiny rips to give me a welcome push onward. Gradually, muscles relaxed, and the constant watchfulness drifted away. I rejoiced that there would be no more portaging today.

On the map, I noted that monument lands extended east of the river for roughly three miles below the Bowlin Camps bridge. Hunting, except for bear hunting with bait or dogs, is allowed on this roughly 1,850-acre block. There are almost twenty thousand additional acres open to hunting east of the river, including a portion of the Three Rivers parcel and the entire noncontiguous Seboeis and Hunt Farm parcels.

Where Little Spring Brook joined the river, there was nothing to indicate the site of the fish hatchery and the critical role it had played in salmon restoration in the early twentieth century. I wondered if someday an interpretive display, or at least an unobtrusive sign, would be erected there. *Could I find any of the ruins?* I wondered. Part of me wanted to stop and explore, but the woods were thick and the day moving along.

Two miles below Little Spring Brook, the river turned sharply to the right. The unimproved Elbow campsite should have been on river left, up a steep bank. While I was climbing up to search for it, the Wavus girls paddled by. I never found the Elbow campsite, or the one called Hathorn Landing, another mile downriver. The latter was shown only on the Thoreau–Wabanaki Trail map, and I later learned that it was no longer being maintained. By now, I was getting anxious as to where I would lay my head. There seemed to be a substantial variation in the visibility and amenities of the East Branch campsites.

After another two miles, I reached the next campsite, Fiske Brook. This one was quite visible, up a slope, in open woods beneath a canopy of old growth trees. Not too surprisingly, it was also occupied. Spacious and roomy, it was perfect for a group, and the Wavus girls had claimed it. The next possibility, Big Seboeis, was three miles downriver, just past the confluence with the Seboeis River.

Onward I went, as the character of the river corridor began to change. Stands of thick spruce, fir, and birch gave way to more open shores. The river wrapped around islands and poked into tiny hidden backwaters. A leisurely current nudged me along, and there was always something to see. As the glaring hot afternoon relented, the river stirred to life. I had a good look at a dark hawk—perhaps a female northern harrier—perched high and wary. Her loud repeated call echoed *kee-kee-kee* across the water.

According to the Maine Natural Areas Program, this was an "exemplary ecosystem," one of the finest of its kind in the state. Known as the Appalachian–Acadian Rivershore ecosystem, it is composed primarily of two natural communities, *silver maple floodplain forest* (rare in Maine) and *hardwood river terrace forest* (imperiled in Maine). Together, these forests and marshes increase biodiversity, provide valuable habitat for waterfowl and wading birds, and work naturally to protect water quality and control seasonal flooding. I found myself drawn to this part of the waterway more than I had anticipated.

The threshold of evening is a magical time. The river and its banks hum with activity before the darkness comes. I drifted on, silent, alert, watching. There, the slice of a beaver cut a shining path through the water before he tail-slapped and dove. Other *plops* came too quickly for me, so my imagination made them what it would—muskrat, otter, or even mink.

Over fifty years ago, in 1968, Congress passed the Wild and Scenic Rivers Act, which legislatively protects individually chosen wild and free-flowing rivers from further development. Currently, in Maine, the only National Wild and Scenic River is the Allagash, but there are many who would like to see the East Branch of the Penobscot similarly protected. Since the 1970s, the East Branch has been recognized as worthy of joining this elite company.

The 1982 Rivers Study, conducted by the Maine Department of Conservation and the National Park Service, identified seven locations within the state where it might be possible to conserve an entire river ecosystem. One of those was the East Branch of the Penobscot and its tributaries.

"These relatively large watersheds," the study elaborated, "are of high significance as undeveloped and interdependent hydrologic units. These sub-basins are characterized by a general lack of major artificial river impoundments, minimal river corridor development, a high degree of hydrologic and ecologic interdependence, and a consistency of resource quality among all segments."

Beyond the science, there is more, an intangible something that sets this place apart.

In the April 7, 1853 edition of the *Cleveland Herald*, a climber of Katahdin, still known only by the mysterious initial "T," penned these words: "I sighed for language to describe the sunrise I beheld this morning. I stood almost upon the summit of Mount Katahdin, 5,000 feet above the waters of the Penobscot and beheld the 'King of Day' crouching like a world of fire at my very feet. Rising majestically from its bed of snowy down, he draws his golden robes around him and walks the blue vault of heaven with a more than reverential tread."

From the heavens high above, well over a century and a half ago, that mysterious writer had gazed down upon the wonders of this river valley. His poetic response was born of sweeping mountain vistas, mine of more intimate discoveries. I had chosen a slower way, the spirit and essence of this place unveiled around the winding bends of trail and river. Both perspectives, however, leave no doubt that this is a land to be preserved for generations to come.

Three waterways share the natural and aesthetic glory. Flowing south, the East Branch is joined first by the Seboeis River, then soon by Wassataquoik Stream. The tumultuous drops of the rocky upper river find an equally stunning counterpart in the golden riverscapes of the lower reaches.

In Maine, a program called Beginning with Habitat (BwH) has recognized the East Branch Penobscot–Seboeis River–Wassataquoik Stream river system as a Focus Area of Statewide Ecological Significance. The goal of the initiative is to conserve wildlife and plant habitat on a landscape scale. Natural resource agencies, including the University of Maine Cooperative Fish and Wildlife Research Unit, the Maine Natural Areas Program, the Maine Department of Inland Fisheries and Wildlife, and the US Fish and Wildlife Service, input their individual data into a geographic information system (GIS).

The resulting maps are used by towns, land trusts, and the state and federal government for decision making. Three key features are prioritized: riparian habitat, in the transitional zone between wetlands and uplands; high-value plant and animal habitats; and undeveloped habitat blocks and connections. All three features occur in abundance within the monument. The focus area stretches from the rivers and floodplain forests to the mountains. "Local bedrock," explains BwH, "creates enriched soils here that support an unusual array of rare natural communities and plants, and the backwaters, pools and water quality of the river systems support a diversity of outstanding aquatic features."

The East Branch is home to a small freshwater mussel called the creeper (*Strophitus undulatus*), typically found in tiny clusters of fewer than ten individuals. This species depends on high water quality and the presence of specific fish and salamander hosts. The national monument provides critical habitat for other rare animals, such as the pygmy snaketail dragonfly, and rare plants, including purple clematis and fragrant woodfern.

By far, the most detailed resource on much of the national monument is the 2014 publication, *East of Katahdin: Ecological Survey of the East Branch Properties of Elliotsville Plantation, Inc., Penobscot*

County, Maine, available in the online DigitalMaine Repository. Ecologist Bart DeWolf, Ph D and a crew of interns spent the summers of 2004 through 2008 completing the fieldwork on seventy-four thousand acres, the vast majority of which later became part of the monument. The study highlighted a broad range of topics from geology and human history to rare and fragile plants and animals. It also included a full cataloging of the natural communities encountered, using the MNAP classification system.

The monument's extensive blocks of contiguous undeveloped habitat provide needed resources for numerous species. The ecological benefits are enhanced by an even larger area of conserved lands adjacent to the monument, including Baxter State Park, the Wassataquoik Public Reserved Land, and Bureau of Parks and Lands parcels. In addition, The Nature Conservancy's Trout Mountain Preserve touches the southwest corner of the monument. "Taken together," DeWolf writes, "these properties encompass an enormous block of diverse habitat: forest, wetlands, ponds, rivers and streams, and alpine and subalpine terrain. The sheer size of the conserved properties is without parallel in Maine."

DeWolf's survey found that roughly half of the surveyed acreage held undisturbed natural communities. The remainder had been logged within the previous twenty years. Some monument lands have a long history of disturbance—due to storms, wildfire, insect damage, and logging—that stretches back almost two centuries. The Wassataquoik Valley experienced at least three extensive wildfires during this time, in 1837 (acreage burned unknown), 1884 (22,000 acres burned), and 1903 (84,480 acres burned, including most of the river valley). Logging of white pine in the Wassataquoik drainage began in 1841, and by the 1880s, other species such as spruce were being cut for both lumber and pulpwood.

The range of successional stages that follow such disturbances are of benefit to many species of wildlife. Edge-loving songbirds abound where blocks meet, and wildlife travel the borders. The young forest provides ideal habitat for ruffed grouse, white-tailed deer, snowshoe hare, and consequently the federally threatened Canada lynx, which feeds primarily on snowshoe hare. Maine has the largest Canada lynx population in the lower 48 states, and numbers are growing. As additional disturbances occur and forests grow back, lucky visitors may catch a glimpse of this shy, medium-sized cat, whose large tufted ears, intent gaze, and striking appearance are an unforgettable sight.

Reclining in the canoe seat, my gaze wandered through open, airy woods, far over a carpet of verdant green. In the parklike environment, it felt as though I could breathe deeply once more. The grassy shoreline was brightened by splotches of color—spikes of crimson cardinal flower and yellow swamp candle, the shy white morning glory on its vine, and the nodding heads of Canada lilies. The buzz of insects droned in the background. The matriarchs of this tranquil scene were the majestic silver maple. Clusters of trunks branched into wide crowns, their arms stretching out toward the river. The leaves were constantly stirring, flickering emerald green above, silvery white below.

In places, I glided beneath the arching branches like a benediction.

The juncture with the Seboeis River was rather unremarkable amid the winding and weaving of the waterway. Not far past that point, I began to hunt for the next campsite.

Whew! Gazing straight ahead downriver, where the sleepy river turned left, was an unmistakable campsite. I smiled with relief. There was a sign and the outline of a picnic table. The canoe scraped gently to a stop and I stepped out stiffly. Up a short path behind the Big Seboeis campsite, I discovered a clean and spacious privy, along a well-worn hiking trail. I had stumbled upon civilization!

The map showed the trail connecting to the Old Telos Tote Road. From the privy, it would be a 4.4-mile hike each way to climb Deasey Mountain to the historic fire cab, via the Werler Trail.

The view of the river from the campsite was backed by the rugged contours of Lunksoos Mountain. In both directions, the panorama of shoreline was overhung by maple and birch. It looked like an Eden for wildlife. Dark and shaded now, I knew from experience that morning would bring sunlight flooding in.

When I awoke, it was the last day of July. A hint of sunrise glowed on the horizon. I sleepily gathered journal and binoculars and settled with a cup of coffee among the roots of a yellow birch overlooking the river. Two families of Canada geese drifted gracefully toward the far shore. Downriver, mist hovered over swirls of dark water. I sat, patiently watching and waiting.

In time, sunlight touched the trees, and the mountain's skirt of cloud was put away. Movement flashed upriver and down. Sounds echoed from the forest. Kingfishers squabbled, swooping to fish, then lighting on branches to catch the morning sun. Brown spotted sandpipers scurried along in spurts, tails bobbing, pecking the sand, a constant whirl of energy. From upriver came the strong, steady approach of a great blue heron. Unmistakable in flight, its powerful wings undulated up and down, with long, long legs stretching straight out behind. Woodpeckers pecked and drummed unseen behind me.

At last, I stood, gingerly, on stiff, numb legs, to fetch a trail bar. Returning to my lookout, I saw a dark something come to the river. My heart raced. Then there were two—wary shadows in the tangled shoreline growth. They must have seen or smelled or sensed me and immediately disappeared. Otter, perhaps, or more likely mink. Dark and far too agile for beaver.

I waited a very long time, hoping that they would return.

When they did not, I turned to the chore of packing up camp once more. In the privy, a sign invited paddlers to stop by Lunksoos Camps, three miles downstream, a forty-five-minute paddle. *We have potable water at a hand pump beside the lodge, a short walk up from the boat launch.* This gesture of kindness was much appreciated, the human touch and voice a welcome change after the solitude of past days. There had not been much in the way of signage coming down the river.

I would visit Lunksoos next. Rich in history, it was a place with many stories to tell.

CHAPTER 15

JOURNEY'S END

To finish the moment, to find the journey's end in every step of the road, to live the greatest number of good hours, is wisdom.

—Ralph Waldo Emerson

I drifted, watching delicate strands of underwater grass wave with the slow pulse of the current. Above the water, not a breath of wind stirred, and the surface was like glass. Before me spread a painter's canvas. The river meandered away under the sheltering arms of the silver maple, then bent to vanish around a corner. Brilliant sun flooded the grassy banks, which gave way in places to stands of spruce and fir, their textures and colors reflected perfectly in the mirror of the river.

The solitude was complete, but I did not feel alone. Around and within me, I imagined the company of the travelers of this land, back through a hundred centuries. I resurrected primal forests, as yet untouched by human hands. Stood in awe to watch as the first settlers arrived to carve out farmsteads along these unknown shores. Even deeper within the mists of time, I glimpsed the rhythms of the Wabanaki and the land, and beyond, the shadows of other ancient peoples that hover at the edges of our knowledge. There are, within and very near the monument, sites that indicate these rivers and streams have been used for the last eight thousand years.

European settlement of the area began in the early 1830s, not long after Maine achieved statehood. Much of the information that follows is drawn from an unpublished manuscript generously shared by John W. Neff. During this era, two key roads were constructed. The Military Road, completed in 1832, roughly paralleled future Interstate 95 on the east. It ran northward and slightly eastward from Mattawamkeag to a new military border outpost in Houlton. The Aroostook Road branched off the Military Road near its start and ran northward and slightly westward to Patten and beyond.

Where the roads led, settlers quickly followed. The Aroostook Road reached Sherman in 1831, and, by 1832, the first homesteads and farms were established there and in nearby Stacyville. Sometime in those early years, a rough road was cut through seven miles of wilderness from Stacyville to the East Branch. Near its halfway point, one entered T3 R7 WELS. Nearly two hundred years later, as I neared Lunksoos, I was just about in the center of the township still known as T3 R7.

In March 1830, a partnership of four men had purchased this township. One of those partners, a merchant named Charles Bonapart Hunt, had an older brother with a true pioneering spirit. William Harmon Hunt probably first heard about the area from Charles, but it is intriguing to wonder if he had also read the narrative of a 1793 surveying expedition that ascended the East Branch.

With Wabanaki guides, the expedition had traveled upriver from just above Bangor on the Penobscot River, all the way to the Matagamon lakes. In addition to gathering geological and botanical information and locating potential mill sites, they had another crucial mission. "They were further charged," Neff explains, "with laying out a boundary line six miles to the east and parallel to the East Branch to be reserved for 'the Indians.'"

The precise field notes of expedition co-leader Jonathan Maynard were later used by cartographer Osgood Carleton in creating his renowned 1795 map of the District of Maine. Neff writes, "Clearly shown (on the Carleton map) is the six-mile wide strip of land reserved for 'the Indians' to the east of the river, intended to reach all the way from Old Town to Grand Lake Matagamon." This reserved tribal land was never shown on later maps. "Sadly," Neff continues, "no explanation is given for the withdrawal of those reserved lands."

Along these serene shores, what was once intended as tribal

land was about to change hands once more. In June 1831, William Harmon Hunt bought his brother's share of township T3 R7. In 1832, he and a friend, Hiram Dacey, became the first nonnative inhabitants to build homes along the East Branch. Whether they floated down-river from the Seboeis on a homemade raft, as family legend suggests, or took the new road from Stacyville, is not known. Arriving in the river valley, they settled about two miles apart. Dacey's farm was a mile above the mouth of Wassataquoik Stream and Hunt's a mile below.

By the late 1830s, the first travelers were trickling into the river valley, just a drop or two of the deluge that would continue through almost a century of scientific exploration, adventuring, and timber

One of fifty photographs taken by Miss Rose Hollingworth during an 1886 Appalachian Mountain Club trip to the "Ktaadn" Basin (LS65.48. Driving a horse-drawn wagon up Wassataquoik Stream road, Maine, by Rose Hollingsworth, August 1886. Appalachian Mountain Club Library & Archives)

harvesting. For over seventy years, from 1841 to 1914, logging in the Wassataquoik valley area would at times bring hundreds of men and horses to these woods. Crews would fell timber in the deep snow and ice of winter. After the spring melt, with the rivers running high, would come the log drives that Edmund Ware Smith called "the most difficult and dramatic of Maine's lumbering history."

The two farms supplied the men and livestock with potatoes, wheat, hay, and other crops. Across the river, the tote road that followed Wassataquoik Stream gradually crept farther up the valley. Signs of civilization began to appear, with logging camps and more than thirty dams eventually scattered along the way. A 2016 survey on lands that would soon become part of the national monument uncovered many traces of this bustling era. In his *Report of Wassataquoik Exploratory Trips, 2016*, Bart DeWolf describes finding stone and

The Lunksoos cable ferry, operated from 1892 to 1922
(Courtesy of Patten Lumbermen's Museum)

wooden dam cribbing, a wagon wheel rim and logging sledge runner, an iron chain and spike, and testaments to everyday life, like a lantern base and part of an old bean pot.

As time passed, the farms became popular starting points for climbing Katahdin. A succession of public accommodations—guest houses, a sporting camp, and even a hotel—came and went at the two locations. Both had the advantage of being situated at natural river fords, where hikers would cross the East Branch to take the Wassataquoik Tote Road toward Katahdin.

C.R. Patterson, who by then owned Hunt Farm, purchased Hiram Dacey's property in 1881. He built a road connecting the two farms, and, in 1892, began operating a ferry at Dacey's. It remained in use until 1922. A thick steel cable stretched from bank to bank, between two anchor trees. Attached to the cable was a wooden raft that transported people, horses, wagons, and other supplies across the river.

Lunksoos Camps, constructed in 1895 at the former site of Dacey's farm, was the first true sporting camp in the region. Its name, historically pronounced *lunk-a-soo*, is believed to come from the Wabanaki word for mountain lion. Mountain lions once roamed the region. In his 1857 account, Thoreau reports that the scream of a cougar had recently been heard near "Ktaadn," not far from where he and his companions stood along the East Branch. Hunched over, they keenly examined a mysterious track in a hollow of rock filled with grass and earth. Joe Polis believed it may have been that of a mountain lion.

Despite a long chronicle of tragedy and perseverance, the business endured. After a 1908 fire, Lunksoos was rebuilt in 1910. The present lodge was constructed in the 1950s and four cabins added in the 1990s. Nowadays, Lunksoos Camps remains an outpost along the secluded river.

My first glimpse of the Lunksoos boat landing was a welcome sight. Beyond, a large field was sprinkled with bright tents and drying gear. The Wavus girls, who had passed by that morning, were making an early camp. They would enjoy a day of rest before continuing their journey to Medway.

I said hello, found the privy, then walked up the short trail to the lodge. There in the yard was an old-fashioned hand pump, a luxury after days of pumping water through my stubborn filter. I took a long drink of fresh cool water and filled my bottles.

The lodge was smaller than I expected, a simple one-story square of log and slab, freshly stained a warm shade of brown. It sat up on pilings, and a high set of stairs led up to a screened porch. The door, trimmed in barn red, was unlocked. Inside, I discovered a hand-written note welcoming visitors. There was no one around, but I plopped down in a chair, away from the bugs, to enjoy my lunch. Looking west through the wide porch windows, I could clearly see Katahdin's majestic summit.

The camp's guest book was filled with enthusiastic comments from the educators, guides, filmmakers, and volunteers who had come to experience their new national monument, hosted by Elliotsville Foundation Recreation Managers, Susan and Mark Adams. I was disappointed to have missed meeting the couple, especially given their pivotal role in caring for monument lands. Their work, begun in the early Elliotsville Plantation days, continues in partnership with the National Park Service.

Over the years, Susan and Mark have constructed, improved, and maintained trails, campsites, vault toilets, and even the hand pump that had so thrilled me. They inaugurated several ongoing annual community events, like Stars over Katahdin and the Fiddlers and Fiddlehead Festival, that connect people with the Katahdin region. In addition, Susan volunteers as the coordinator of the NPS Volunteers-in-Parks program at the monument. Perhaps I would one day meet her, as I hoped to volunteer in the national monument in the future.

Through the early twentieth century, the East Branch continued to be the preferred gateway to the Katahdin region. Geologists, botanists, artists, and even a future US president came this way. Painter Frederic Church, a college student named Teddy Roosevelt, and countless others whose names are less familiar. Of them all, perhaps none was more impacted by the experience than future Maine Governor Percival P. Baxter. We last left Baxter in early 1921, as the newly elected President of the Maine Senate, avidly pursuing his goal of creating Mount Katahdin State Park to honor Maine's centennial. The summer before, in August 1920, Baxter had summited Katahdin for the first time, as part of a large expedition. The group included businessmen, politicians, journalists, the state's Fish and Game Commissioner, and its Chief Game Warden, as well as the Bangor & Aroostook Railroad official responsible for producing the annual publication *In the Maine Woods*. Their goal—to gather information and enlist support for the establishment of the proposed centennial park—was timely.

The climbers spent the night at Lunksoos, before heading up along the Wassataquoik Tote Road. They were led by none other than Roy Dudley, the Chimney Pond guide famous for his yarns about Pamola. After climbing Pamola Peak and crossing the harrowing Knife Edge, Baxter reached the peak that would one day be named for him. He returned committed to preserving Katahdin at all costs.

"…Baxter's effort now took on the flavor of a personal crusade," writes John W. Neff, in *Katahdin: An Historic Journey*. "The die was cast. The effort would become one of the central themes of his political and personal agenda." Baxter long remembered the importance of the moment when he stood upon the almost mile-high summit, writing eleven years later, "While I was there that day I said to myself, 'This shall belong to Maine if I live.'"

And so, momentum grew and became ever more vocal. One wonders what might have been accomplished legislatively if Baxter's political path had not taken a drastic, unforeseen turn. On January 31, 1921, after just twenty-six days in office, Governor Frederic H. Parkhurst became ill and unexpectedly died. The state does not have the position of lieutenant governor, so the president of the Maine Senate is next in succession. Baxter, therefore, was immediately sworn in as the 53rd Governor of Maine.

Debate continued as the legislation to create the state park was officially introduced in late February. Those in favor spoke of preserving magnificent Katahdin, with its forests, wildlife, and recreational potential, for future generations. Those opposed feared the taking of lands by eminent domain and the high costs of land acquisition and road building. They argued that the lands were already available for use by the people of Maine. Many of these arguments would be echoed almost a century later, when Roxanne Quimby introduced her vision for a new Maine national park.

As governor, Baxter felt compelled to take a more conservative view of the economic impacts of the park bill. He withdrew his support for the $100,000 appropriation for land purchases, and ultimately, the bill was defeated. Although Baxter continued to strongly advocate for the preservation of Katahdin, five more bills to establish a state or federal park failed over the next few years. The only victory came in 1921, when Willis E. Parsons, who had climbed Katahdin with Baxter the year before, used his authority as Maine's Inland Fish and Game Commissioner to establish what grew into a ninety-thousand-acre game preserve surrounding Katahdin.

After serving a second two-year term as governor, Baxter did not seek reelection and left office in January 1925. According to Neff, that was the year Baxter "gave up on the effort to create a park by legislative action and decided the only way open was to buy the land himself and give it to the state."

If his vision were to become a reality, Baxter alone would have to make it happen. Luckily, he had the financial resources to accomplish his lofty goal. His first purchase, a partial interest in a parcel that included Katahdin, became the foundation of the new park when Baxter donated it to the State of Maine on March 3, 1931. By October 1931, after months of complicated negotiations, Baxter was able to transfer to the state full title to 5,960 acres, which the Maine legislature designated in early 1933 as Baxter State Park.

Baxter dedicated the rest of his life to expanding the park. That he accomplished all that he did without the legal tools of condemnation and eminent domain is amazing. Hakola praises Baxter's patience and creativity. At times, he pursued individual tracts for over two decades, paid more than the land was worth, or purchased higher value timberlands to trade for parcels that he truly wanted. Baxter purchased twenty-eight tracts, totaling more than two hundred thousand acres, the last in 1962 at the age of eighty-five. In addition, he left a trust of more than $10 million for future park maintenance and management.

The vision and generosity that preserved Baxter State Park and

Katahdin Woods and Waters National Monument are reflected in a multitude of other, smaller but no less precious, donations of land across the state. The value of these gifts—given to communities, land trusts, or parks—will continue to grow. Perhaps only future generations will fully appreciate their worth. As Baxter said of his legacy, "Man is born to die. His works are short-lived. Buildings crumble, monuments decay, and wealth vanishes, but Katahdin in all its glory forever shall remain the mountain of the people of Maine."

Back in my canoe down at the boat landing, I checked the map. Lunksoos Camps was just inside the southern end of the monument's large main parcel. Following the river, I would leave, then soon rejoin the monument at the Hunt Farm parcel on river left.

Downstream, the river began to deepen and stir, and I glimpsed the shadowy outlines of large rocks hovering below. A mile below Lunksoos, the wide, sparkling waters of Wassataquoik Stream came bubbling in on river right. Here at its mouth, the stream appeared good-natured, but it also has a wild side. From the Baxter State Park boundary, this lively tributary plummets five hundred feet in fourteen miles, a descent twice as steep as that of the upper East Branch.

In 1939, the Wassataquoik Valley was the dramatic setting for a life-and-death struggle that captivated the nation. After summiting Katahdin on the afternoon of July 17th, twelve-year-old Donn Fendler parted ways with the older friend with whom he was hiking. Alone, he headed down to meet his father and brothers, still on their way to the peak. Somewhere in the swirling cloud and blasting wind, he lost the trail. Above tree line, conditions quickly deteriorated. Pummeled by sleet and hail, Fendler wisely chose to keep moving, as forty-mile-per-hour winds howled. By morning, the temperature would be below forty degrees.

Drawing upon his scout training, prayers, and a natural optimism, Fendler encouraged himself to stay calm. Having given his sweatshirt to his friend, Donn wore only jeans, sneakers, and a thin, flannel-lined jacket. That he survived may have been a miracle, but much credit must go to Donn's resiliency and outlook. Buoyed by the perpetual thought that a hiker or fisherman might be just around the next bend, Donn often reminded himself that "a fellow" just needed to keep his head.

On the second day, Donn happened upon a small brook and decided to follow it downstream, no matter what. His feet were now too swollen to wear his tattered sneakers, so he abandoned them. The brook grew gradually larger, then joined Wassataquoik Stream. On the third day, Donn tried to toss his soaked jeans across a gap between rocks, but they slipped into the rushing water and were gone, too. Eating nothing but berries, he went on. On the ninth day, the land began to open out into a low floodplain.

Weak and disoriented, stumbling, falling, and getting up once more, Donn somehow made it to the East Branch. Across from him, on the far shore, stood a cabin. It was Lunksoos Camps. There, after wandering an estimated eighty miles, Donn Fendler was saved.

When my son Taylor was thirteen, we climbed Katahdin for the first time. After our eleven-hour ascent and descent—via the Abol and Hunt trails—we could hardly move the next morning. But we could read. At the park's visitor center, we purchased Fendler's book, *Lost on a Mountain in Maine.* By the end of the day, back at our campsite, we had both read it straight through.

Before continuing my river journey, I pulled out the map. Thoreau's "Hemlock Tea Camp" was shown just downstream of the Wassataquoik confluence on river right. Halfheartedly, I searched for some indication of the spot where Joe Polis had brewed another flavor of tea. By now, I was longing for some tangible evidence of all this monument history. There had been ferries and farms, and a bunch of tea-drinking, but so far nothing to see from the river. I yearned to explore, and touch, some remnant of the monument's alluring past.

A mile below Wassataquoik Stream, with monument lands once more adjacent to the river, I began to search for the site of the former Hunt Farm. It was not hard to find. At a place where the river bent to the right, there was the spot, no doubt about it. The left bank rose in a high sandy bluff that made a very distinctive landmark.

In many ways, this had been an attractive location for a pioneer homestead. In fact, Neff believes that Hunt may well have chosen this location after reading Jonathon Maynard's account of the 1793 surveying expedition. Neff writes, "On September 3, after noting an excellent mill site at today's Whetstone Falls, they reached the future site of Hunt Farm. Of special interest to our story is Maynard's discovery there of a mile of a 'mostly fine intervale' [a low-lying tract of land along a river] and an area of 'shoal' [a shallow place]." In addition to the natural ford and intervale, the high bluff on a bend would have afforded Hunt a broad view up and down the river.

Hunt's had been the larger of the two farms, comprising about a hundred acres of cleared land. Thanks to an eyewitness report from one of the first guests, we have a clear snapshot of its early days. That visitor was Charles Thomas Jackson, Maine's first state geologist. In *Katahdin: An Historic Journey*, Neff gives us a look at Hunt Farm through Jackson's eyes.

"When Jackson and his party stayed there in October 1837, he reported that the Hunt Farm was well-established and that Hunt

Stopping to explore near the site of the former Hunt Farm

had brought the soil to an excellent state of cultivation. Hunt had built his one and a half-story farmhouse out of hand-hewn squared logs, boarded over. A large kitchen, several fireplaces, outbuildings, and a large barn offered ample space. Jackson added that Hunt had raised 100 bushels of wheat and an abundance of potatoes and hay— some of which was sold to the loggers for the animals they kept at the logging camps deeper in the wilderness."

Eager to explore, I would have landed, but I spotted a cabin perched atop the high bank. I wanted to respect the privacy of the owners and hesitated to stop after all. I felt as though I were missing my last chance. The Hunt Farm parcel was the last chunk of the monument I would see. Just a short distance downriver, I would leave Katahdin Woods and Waters for good, for this trip anyway.

As I rounded the bend, I could see a long pebble beach stretching along the left shore, well below the cabin. I headed straight for it and felt comfortable pulling my boat up on shore. The river here was broad and shallow. The beach was composed of a pleasing medley of stones, some rounded, some irregular, in shades of gray, white, pink, and brown. The beach flowed seamlessly into the river, extending across toward the far bank. Here, the subtle colors of the stones came to life, magnified by the clear water.

The first thing that caught my eye was an old worn piece of brick, pitted with age. At last, here was something I could touch and hold, visible evidence of those who had dwelt here long ago. Then I spotted some glimmers of white in the shallows, wavering brightly against the darker backdrop of stones. Quickly, I waded out and stooped to pick up one of the objects. It was a shard of white pottery, part of a saucer or plate, yet another connection with the past.

By then, my heart was racing. Looking intently, I scoured the shore, finding piece after piece of broken pottery scattered along the beach. One of the first had part of an intricate design with an embellished crest on a fine, shiny white background. I held the delicate fragment and read, below the crest, the letters "& G. MEAK," "ANLEY," and "GLAN." Hanley, England, perhaps?

It was like a treasure hunt.

There was part of a mixing bowl, with alternating dark- and light-blue stripes, chunks of stoneware crocks, and the rim of a white

One of many pottery fragments found near the Hunt Farm site—the writing on this piece of white ironstone led to a manufacturer in Hanley, England

bowl, its scalloped edge rimmed with tiny dots. Later, I would share my photos with archaeologist Tim Dinsmore, who dated most of my finds to the mid- to late-nineteenth century. A piece of thick white-ware with a sponge blue decoration was potentially old enough to have come to the farm with the Hunt family in the early 1830s.

The writing on two of the pieces was enough for Dinsmore to locate the manufacturer. The white ironstone pottery had been made by J. & G. Meakin, of Hanley, England. Their potter's mark, which had changed over the years, could be used to date the pieces. This version of the design, with "the royal arms flanked by two lions rampant," dated the pieces to between 1891 and 1907. Perhaps this had been the dishware used in the dining room of the Matagamon House, a small turn-of-the-century hotel that had once stood upon the bluff. The dates were right.

Carefully, I photographed and returned each artifact to its resting place, leaving everything just as I had found it. I sincerely hoped that future visitors would do the same.

So, with my departure from Katahdin Woods and Waters fast approaching, I had uncovered a window into the past after all. A reminder of the years when Hunt Farm had seen visits from Frederic Church, the Reverend Marcus Keep, and many others. Even Thoreau had stopped there, hoping to buy some sugar. The family was away but he had talked with some workers cutting hay on the farm.

This busy era was long gone, but it cheered me to know that it would not be forgotten.

Two miles below Hunt Farm waited Whetstone Falls, comprised of two Class II+ to Class III rapids. The time had come to refocus my attention on running whitewater. Making sure that my gear was all well secured, I slid the canoe back into the water and hopped in. Not far along, near the monument boundary, a rocket of diving motion caught my eye. A bald eagle plunged from the sky toward a flurry of ducks scurrying along the surface. Somehow, he missed, and I did not see him return.

Two sets of rapids at Whetstone Falls meant two portage trails and two opportunities for scouting.

The portage around the first, on river right, was short and clear. The trail passed by an attractive campsite, not mentioned on any of the maps. A large, well-crafted fire pit was the centerpiece of a square of log seats. Blueberry bushes hung plump with fruit. From the campsite, a substantial stone stairway led down to a small beach. In my journal, my enthusiasm and exhilaration for this spot shine through.

Gonna run this one, I wrote, and I did. *Ran from left of center to center like a charm, great standing waves, not a rock touched.* A moment of redemption for sure.

The second rapid promised to be far more complicated. It began just above the Whetstone Falls Bridge and continued underneath it and beyond. This was the bridge where my parents and I had pulled over on our drive along Swift Brook Road to reach the Loop Road, weeks before. I recalled the thrill of coming across our first official monument sign and pondering the unexplored river below.

The portage here was on river left, but the right shore offered a fine opportunity for scouting. A large peninsula of rock angled far out into the river, the quiet water behind it safely sheltered. I tied up the boat and pulled myself high up and over the rocks, until I could look downriver, beyond the bridge, to the end of the whitewater. There looked to be more rock than water under the bridge. Plus, bridges add an extra layer of complexity to any rapid. I decided to walk this one, at least until I got around the bridge.

Back in the canoe, I edged into the current and cautiously crossed to a sand beach just before the bridge. As I clambered over a wide barricade of large boulders to cross the road, two men rode up, one on a four-wheeler and one on a dirt bike. They didn't have much to say, but then again, I didn't either.

The monument map shows only a picnic area here, but other sources mentioned camping, although no fires were allowed. Because of the road access, I did not even consider staying. Below, there were no more official campsites, so it would be a stealth camp for me on this last night out.

My audience showed no sign of moving on. The two men had driven down to the boat launch and were lounging around, chatting and unabashedly watching me. Hastily, I reloaded the canoe. Downstream, I thought I could pick out some good lines through the remainder of the whitewater. I walked the boat out to a strategic spot, then hopped in, paddle poised for action.

All went well, for which I was especially thankful.

Emerging safely into quiet water below, I knew I could relax. From Whetstone Falls, it was 12.5 miles to the Grindstone Falls picnic area, where I planned to meet my parents at noon the following day. The only significant rapid between here and there was Class II Crowfoot Rapids, ten miles away. It was already late afternoon, so that challenge would come tomorrow.

I ended up paddling five more miles that evening, mostly through land owned by the Butler Conservation Fund. In 2016, this family funded charitable foundation had purchased 4,342 acres along both shores of a continuous 8.6-mile stretch of the East Branch.

As I passed through in the summer of 2018, there was nothing to indicate the new ownership. The following year, in 2019, the foundation opened a first-class facility here. Called Penobscot River

Trails, it provides recreational access to this entire section of the river. Depending on the season, more than fifteen miles of old tote roads and new gravel trails are available for hiking, biking, cross-country skiing, or snowshoeing. There is more, too—a welcome center, warming huts, restrooms, hand carry boat launches, and rental of equipment, including canoes and kayaks.

The wide and placid river presented few rocks and just enough mellow whitewater to keep me awake and alert. As Goose and Maverick had, I saw a "plethora" of eagles along this segment. There is something sacred and empowering about accompanying an eagle down a wild river, as the mighty bird repeatedly launches from above, the rush of wings sensed as well as heard.

I found my evening camp on Brown Island, which looked from the map to be the largest of the midstream islands along this stretch. I set up the tent in a low, dry, flat sandy spot that reminded me of Goose and Maverick's "Bear Haven" on Webster Brook, minus the bear. I cooked my last dinner and finished the last O. Henry story. Darkness descended upon the river, and upon my last night.

The next morning, I peeked out of my tent at a very early hour. I wanted to be sure to make the rendezvous on time. The glorious prelude of the rising sun tinted the sky a primrose pink. The moon lingered over camp, keeping watch a little longer, and a chorus of songbirds serenaded me. My island in the river had slept peacefully. To my knowledge, no one and no creature had come in the night.

Well before seven, I bid farewell to Brown Island. Seven miles of river remained, and the current pushed me along toward my reunion with family. Rain showers were forecast for later, but for now, the sun could be seen rising to take the place of the moon. A family of mergansers cruised silently along the dark shaded shore. On the sunny side, these final morning miles were graced with favorite flowers, morning glory, swamp milkweed, cardinal flower, and swamp candle.

About halfway along, however, the sounds of heavy machinery began to penetrate the idyllic scene. A discordant backup alarm was accompanied by pounding, squealing, and a constant background hum and rattle. By eight, I reached the Hay Brook boat landing, where I discovered the source of the racket, a backhoe toiling in the dirt. There were other reminders that my solitude had ended—a windsock, channel markers, and an encounter with a friendly father and his young son in an old red kayak.

In another mile, I breezed through easy Class II Crowfoot Rapids, running it right down the center. In another mile, just before a railroad bridge, I spotted thick rusty chains encircling some island rocks. Underwater lurked heavy sunken timbers in a framework held together by iron spikes. I poked around, gazing down through the brown water at this evidence of the old-time log drives, and a shiver went down my spine. For some reason, I thought of the men who had given their lives on the river.

By ten in the morning, my journey was at last finished. Just before the rest area, I stopped to check out the small building housing the USGS Grindstone Gaging Station. This station measures East Branch streamflow and water levels and is a key resource for canoe trip planning. Thankfully, the rest area came before Grindstone Falls. The AMC river guide recommends running this half-mile-long Class

Journey's end, just above Grindstone Falls, nine miles from the confluence with the West Branch in Medway

III–IV rapid with an empty boat. After getting a thorough look at it, I knew that I would not have attempted it.

Landing in a sandy spot and hauling my canoe up the bank, I spread my gear to dry in the sun. I took lots of photos of myself, posing proudly with my paddle raised in victory, until I got a good one. Then, there was nothing to do but wait for my parents, who would end up arriving right at noon, ready to listen to a multitude of stories. I sat with my back against a sun-warmed rock and let my thoughts drift with the murmur of the river.

What an adventure it had been! I had accomplished what I set out to do and done it well enough. The gifts of nature had come, often with an air of serendipity, and I had paused to appreciate them. I had fellowshipped with wild creatures and the people of the past, seen anew the intricacy and drama of God's creation, and tested my strength, endurance, and resiliency. I had breathed deeply and thought deeply and renewed my soul in hidden corners that few will ever see. It had been a good visit home.

EPILOGUE

The future belongs to those who believe in the beauty of their dreams.

—**Eleanor Roosevelt**

For those with a soul for the wilderness, the journey never ends when the gear is put away. How much more is that true for the writer, who will relive and recreate each bend of trail and river.

Back home, I reunited with loved ones and took up the busy threads of life. As always, I was a bit amazed to find the world unchanged, when I was not. The spirit of wild places was still within me, and I did not want to let it go. There, I had affirmed my true self, the one I rediscover on each long journey. The river makes me stronger, surer, and more thankful, awes me and empowers me. All this I would strive to capture in words during the months ahead. There were so many stories to tell.

I could not know it then, but those stories would bring me back to Katahdin Woods and Waters and take me down an unexpected path. In the late spring of 2019, by then immersed in writing, I came up for an IAT gathering and then the Fiddlers and Fiddlehead Festival. As the months went by, I was beginning to sense a more enduring call to this place. Casually, I began to look around at real estate, just for fun.

That summer, my new house found me. Located in Patten, it sits along the road to the northern entrances of both the monument and Baxter. It is an honest, old-fashioned, two-story farmhouse with a yard of lilac, columbine, and ancient apple trees. Amish buggies *clip-clop* past as I tend the garden, and time seems to fall away. Before too long, I hope to make this my fulltime home in retirement.

Like my dreams, the future of the monument is bright with promise. Gradually, progress is being made. The highway signs have gone up. New trails invite exploration, and there are eight more tent sites being constructed at Lunksoos, thanks to a grant from L.L. Bean. Two interpretive ranger positions have been approved for the 2020 season, and a bird checklist and dark-sky guide are now available. Many questions about the future may remain unanswered, but this is not necessarily bad news. The deliberate pace of planning has allowed ample time for public input and reflection.

The National Park Service will soon release its Framework for Management of Katahdin Woods and Waters. This document is designed to provide the "overarching vision" for future work and activities, while allowing for fluid decision-making. In June 2019, I participated in a public comment session on the draft. That was my first look at the proposed management matrix and map.

The map and matrix divide monument lands into five zones, based on factors like location, topography, physical features, and anticipated usage. These zones are: Monument Gateway, Developed Recreation, River Corridor, Non-Intensive Use, and Backcountry. Within each zone, the matrix addresses desired visitor experiences and resource conditions. Building on those desires, it then outlines appropriate types of development, management activities, and visitor activities for each zone. For example, in the Monument Gateway, visitors might expect to be welcomed with paved parking areas, restrooms, interpretive exhibits, maps, and other infrastructure and activities for orientation and education.

Elliotsville Foundation Inc. remains an extremely active partner in monument operations and improvements. Back in 2016, the Quimby family foundation gave more than the $80 million worth of land. They also provided a $20 million endowment for "initial operational and infrastructure costs" and pledged an additional $20 million for "future funding." When the deeds conveying the land were written, Elliotsville Plantation Inc. retained certain reserved rights that could be exercised through August 12, 2023. These allow for the potential construction of visitor contact stations, boat launches, trails, roads, and parking areas in specifically designated areas, all on the east side of the East Branch.

The endowment is meant to fund what Lucas St. Clair calls the "margin of excellence," helping the already resourceful National Park Service to better accomplish its vision. At times that means paying for the mundane, like road grading or vault toilets. However, the endowment also heavily supports the work of the Friends of Katahdin Woods and Waters, who produce maps and publications, sponsor community events, and engage students and educators in a thriving place-based learning program.

There is another vital project on the horizon.

"Out of all the reserved rights," I asked Lucas St. Clair, "what are you considering doing?"

"We are going to build a visitor center," he answered. "Visitors are arriving with certain expectations that are not always being met. We want people to understand where they are and what they are going to see. To orient them to the landscape and educate them on what's happened to it from a geological perspective, from a human perspective, from an industrial perspective, and from a conservation perspective. We want them to see that whole evolution to deepen their understanding."

The timeline for construction of the visitor center is uncertain. There are no architectural drawings or regulatory permits yet. The planned location is close to Lunksoos Camps. To reach the facility, visitors driving west from Stacyville toward the Loop Road will turn off Swift Brook Road onto access roads that must still be built, along with parking areas, hardscaping, landscaping, and more.

Currently, COVID-19 restrictions are dramatically slowing the entire process, and the clock is ticking. The reserved rights that allow for the construction expire in August 2023. There is also fundraising to consider. Half of the funding for the facility will come from Elliotsville Foundation and half from an anticipated capital campaign.

Despite these hurdles, St. Clair is optimistic. Hearing him describe the vision for the building, I am enthralled and can almost see it. The concept sounds so in harmony with the land.

"We're working closely with the four federally recognized native tribes in Maine to help inform the design," St. Clair elaborates. "We want it to be forward facing, thinking about how buildings can be constructed with the lightest impact on the land. It'll be off grid of course, use little energy, and be built from local materials."

"Will there be live craft demonstrations?" I ask, immediately thinking of the fine, intricately woven brown ash and sweetgrass baskets of the Wabanaki and the contemporary artisans who create them. The answer is yes. In addition, there will be exhibits of indigenous artwork and perhaps even elements of Wabanaki art incorporated into the design of the building. For me, this connection of the present with the past seems crucial to the understanding of this place and the integrity of its future.

When the basket makers come, they may be women or men, likely Penobscot or Passamaquoddy, or possibly Maliseet or Micmac. As their hands deftly shape the thin ash splints around wooden forms worn with age, they will likely share a troubling story. Their age-old craft faces a grave and growing environmental threat, one that took on new urgency in the year of my trip.

For over a decade, Maine's basket makers had been tracking the relentless approach of an invasive beetle called the Emerald Ash Borer. This Asian native is a shiny metallic green, half an inch long, and shaped like a grain of rice on steroids. The destructive beetle attacks all species of ash, including the brown or black ash (*Fraxinus nigra*) used in basketmaking. Since first detected in Michigan in 2002, the Emerald Ash Borer has killed tens of millions of trees in the United States.

In 2018, the devastating news came. The Emerald Ash Borer had been discovered at both ends of the state, in Aroostook County in the north and in York County in the south. Since then, the infested region has been gradually expanding. The state has responded vigorously, even releasing tiny non-stinging parasitic wasps that attack and kill the beetle's eggs and larvae. Maine also has an official ban on the transport of firewood from out of state or from the infested quarantine area. No matter where we live, we can all help in the fight by purchasing firewood locally, rather than bringing it from home.

To date, the monument's brown ash, commonly found in natural communities like the silver maple floodplain forest, have not been affected. The closest quarantine area, in northern Aroostook County, is over sixty miles north of Katahdin Woods and Waters. Still, I ponder what the future of Wabanaki basketry will look like if all the ash trees are one day lost.

Recently, an event hosted by the Abbe Museum featured several nationally recognized Wabanaki basket makers. Seeing the evolution of the craft—the experimentation with new materials, the innovation of styles to match modern needs, and the blending of tradition with individual artistic expression—I came away more hopeful. These artisans, I believe, exemplify the resiliency of the Wabanaki people, and their work, deeply rooted in the spiritual, natural, and economic heritage of the past, will surely endure.

At the eleventh hour for the writing of this book, another major victory was announced. In May 2020, Katahdin Woods and Waters officially became the first Dark Sky Sanctuary east of the Mississippi! This is cause for much rejoicing. The dark skies will be protected, and astrotourism will surely grow. While some facets of the monument experience will take time to develop, stargazing will never be finer than it is today. Looking down the road, the path of an April 8, 2024 total solar eclipse is projected to fall almost directly over the northern end of the monument. I, for one, plan to be in place to view it!

As we part ways, until the next river beckons, the tale will go on. One memorable summer, I went in search of serendipity and found it in abundance. Along the winding way, I heard the voices of those who had gone before, and they stirred my heart and soul. One flowed into another, centered in this land that shelters in the shadow of Katahdin. It is humbling to think that my voice may join that flow, to become part of a story that will last for as long as the mountains stand.

We will end as we began, with the reflections of John Muir. Here, in shining prose, is the very essence of what calls me home to the woods and waters, and always will.

"The sun shines not on us but in us. The rivers flow not past, but through us. Thrilling, tingling, vibrating every fiber and cell of the substance of our bodies, making them glide and sing. The trees wave and the flowers bloom in our bodies as well as our souls, and every bird song, wind song, and tremendous storm song of the rocks in the heart of the mountains is our song, our very own, and sings our love."

ACKNOWLEDGMENTS

By nature, I often choose the solitary path and find it good. There is fulfillment in the quiet glide down misty rose-dawn waters or endless rapt hours in the grip of the keyboard, the words swirling, shifting, then finally settling into rightness. No traveler or writer, though, truly journeys alone.

I relied heavily on the wisdom of those who had gone that way before, especially Zip Kellogg, Dana Cinq-Mars, "Goose," and Johnson Whippie, "Maverick." These were my companions, the ones who buoyed my spirits and brought me safely home. Up north, help often appears at critical moments. For guidance and bountiful hospitality, from cookies and trucks to warm purple sweatshirts, thanks go to Ed and Shirley Raymond, Ray and Leslie Cooley, Bob Johnston, and the Christianson family.

A traveler needs a destination, and I had one of the very finest. Roxanne Quimby, thank you for your gift. Cheers to Lucas St. Clair, who took the vision from its roots to reality, and to all those who are working to make Katahdin Woods and Waters National Monument what it will one day become, especially Superintendent Tim Hudson and the staff of the Friends of Katahdin Woods and Waters.

Then there is the cast of characters (some might call them visionaries) who followed a chain of mountains from Maine through Canada and across a rather large ocean to Europe and beyond. Dick Anderson, Don Hudson, and Earl Raymond, I am honored to have followed a short way in your footsteps.

For a deeper understanding of the region, I turned to a multitude of teachers. They gave generously of their time and expertise to help me get it right, and I am grateful. My esteemed professors included Robert Marvinney, Maine State Geologist; Randy Cross and Shevenell Webb, MDIFW biologists; Dr. Bart DeWolf, ecologist; and John Meader, whose extremely cool business, Northern Stars Planetarium, brings inflatable planetariums into public schools, including mine.

The best historians open windows into the past with curiosity, patience, and exactitude. John Neff, you are indeed one of the best. My words are better because of you. Paul Johnson, retired MDIFW fisheries biologist, wore many hats, most notably making me an assistant detective in researching the history of the fish hatchery. It was a thrill to page through volumes of century-old letters, piecing together the past. Dan and Sandi Day, you brought Jake's Rangers to life for me, until I felt that I had met them, too. I wish I could have.

Sometimes others said it better than I ever could. Thanks go to all those who gave me permission to quote from published works, including Gil Gilpatrick; Elizabeth Hall Harmon; John Neff; George Smith; and the families of Ted Clapp, Lester Hall, and Ed Werler.

The team of Maine Authors Publishing staff and fellow writers is my village, providing the expertise, inspiration, and cheerleading that make this new author life possible. Special thanks this time around to Jennifer and Wendy, my editor and designer, and always to Jane, Jenn, Nikki, Dan, and Lee.

In life and the crazy adventures that it continues to deliver, my parents are my anchor. They advise me, calm me and encourage me, drop me off and pick me up, resupply me, and wait patiently for the writing to be done. Their greatest gift has always been in nurturing the quirky, bookish, independent little girl who has never really changed.

Two friends remain to acknowledge. Without them, *Through Woods & Waters* would not have become the book I envisioned. Katina Daanen, when you said yes to reading my many drafts, as you did with *Upwards*, I was thrilled. Like a sister, you tell it like it is, helping me to see the broad landscape of the moving story and craft the finest details. Arne Aho, words can never do justice to all that you have given to this project. In the maps you drew are the scent of the fir, the pull of the paddle, and the songs of the voyageurs. I will be forever grateful for my cartographer.

REFERENCES

American Whitewater. 2018. "Penobscot, W. Branch, Seboomook Dam to Roll Dam Campsite." https://www.americanwhitewater.org/content/River/detail/id/868/.

Appalachian Mountain Club. 2008. *AMC River Guide: Maine*. Edited by John Fiske. Boston, MA: Appalachian Mountain Club Books.

Baxter State Park Authority. n.d. "The Scientific Forest Management Area (SFMA)." *Baxter State Park*. https://baxterstatepark.org/forest-management/.

Baxter State Park. 2017. "The A.T. and I.A.T.: Special Trails in Baxter State Park." *Wildnotes*, 3.

Beginning with Habitat. n.d. "Focus Areas of Statewide Ecological Significance: East Branch Penobscot-Seboeis River—Wassataquoik Stream." *Maine Department of Agriculture, Conservation and Forestry*. https://www.maine.gov/dacf/mnap/focusarea/east_branch_penobscot_focus_area.pdf.

Bennett, Dean B. 1988. *Maine's Natural Heritage: Rare Species and Unique Natural Features*. Camden, ME: Down East Books.

Bortle, John. 2006. "Gauging Light Pollution: The Bortle Dark-Sky Scale." *Sky and Telescope*. July 18. https://www.skyandtelescope.com/astronomy-resources/light-pollution-and-astronomy-the-bortle-dark-sky-scale/.

Chandler, Laurie Apgar. 2017. *Upwards: The Story of the First Woman to Solo Thru-Paddle the Northern Forest Canoe Trail*. Thomaston, ME: Maine Authors Publishing.

Clapp, Ted. 2013. *Tell Me About the River and Other Stories from the Coast of Maine*. Damariscotta, ME: Old Crow Press.

Cornell Lab of Ornithology. 2019. "All About Birds." https://www. allaboutbirds.org/.

Daanen, Katina. 2019. *The Northern Forest Canoe Trail Through-Paddler's Companion.* 3rd.

DeLorme. 2019. *The Maine Atlas and Gazetteer.* 35th ed. Yarmouth, ME: Garmin Ltd.

DeWolf, B. 2014. *East of Katahdin: Ecological Survey of the East Branch Properties of Elliotsville Plantation, Inc., Penobscot County, Maine.* Elliotsville Plantation, Inc., Portland, ME.

DeWolf, B. 2017. *Report of Wassataquoik Exploratory Trips, 2016.* Maine Woods Forever, Oakland, ME.

Eckstorm, Fannie Hardy, "Maine Indian Legends—undated" (2018). *Fannie Hardy Eckstorm Papers.* Submission 40. https://digitalcommons.library. umaine.edu/eckstorm_papers/40.

Fendler, Donn, as told to Joseph B. Egan. 1978. *Lost on a Mountain in Maine.* New York, NY: Beech Tree Books.

Friends of Katahdin Woods and Waters. 2019. "Katahdin Woods & Waters National Monument Dark Sky Guide." *Friends of Katahdin Woods and Waters.* https://www.friendsofkww.org/wp-content/uploads/2019/10/ Katahdin-Woods-and-Waters-National-Monument-Dark-Sky-Guide-1st-Edition-Friends-of-Katahdin-Woods-and-Waters.pdf.

Friends of Katahdin Woods and Waters. 2018. "Katahdin Woods & Waters National Monument Loop Road Interpretive Map." Northern Geomantics, Inc.

Friends of Katahdin Woods and Waters. 2018. "Katahdin Woods & Waters Waterproof Trail Map." Portland, ME: Map Adventures LLC.

Geller, William W., "Mount Katahdin—March 1853: the Mysteries of an Ascent" (2016). Maine History Documents. 119. https://digitalcommons. library.umaine.edu/mainehistory/119.

Gilpatrick, Gil. 2010. *Allagash: A Journey Through Time on Maine's Legendary Wilderness Waterway.* East Petersburg, PA: Fox Chapel Publishing.

Hakola, Dr. John W. 1981. *Legacy of a Lifetime: The Story of Baxter State Park.* Woolwich, ME: TBW Books.

Hall, Clayton and Jane Thomas, with Elizabeth Hall Harmon. 2013. *Chimney Pond Tales: Yarns Told by Leroy Dudley.* Cumberland Center, ME: The Pamola Press.

Holyoke, John. 2010. "Bear Attacks Unusual, but Not Unknown." *Bangor Daily News*. Sept. 15. http://bangordailynews.com/2010/09/15/outdoors/bear-attacks-unusual-but-not-unknown/.

Huber, J. Parker. 2008. *The Wildest Country: Exploring Thoreau's Maine.* Boston, MA: Appalachian Mountain Club Books.

International Dark-Sky Association. 2019. "International Dark Sky Places." https://www.darksky.org/our-work/conservation/idsp/.

Kellogg, Zip. 1983. *Maine Geographic Canoeing Volume 3: Northern Rivers.* Freeport, ME: DeLorme Publishing Co.

Kendall, David L. 1987. *Glaciers & Granite: A Guide to Maine's Landscape & Geology.* Unity, ME: North Country Press.

Kirkpatrick, Charlotte Hall, ed. 2010. *Katahdin Comrades: The Journals of Lester F. Hall.* Brunswick, ME: High Point Graphics.

Leigh Tillman Facilitation. 2016. "Community Listening Sessions Report of Input." *National Park Service: Katahdin Woods and Waters National Monument.* September. https://www.nps.gov/kaww/getinvolved/upload/NPS-Katahdin-Woods-and-Waters-Community-Listening-Sessions-Report-of-Input-September-2016-1-w-post-publ-comments.pdf.

Levin, Ted. 2012. "The Staying Power of Snapping Turtles." *Audubon.* March-April. https://www.audubon.org/magazine/march-april-2012/the-staying-power-snapping-turtles.

Maine Center for Invasive Aquatic Plants. 2007. "Maine Field Guide to Invasive Aquatic Plants and Their Common Native Look Alikes." *Lake Stewards of Maine.* https://lakestewardsofmaine.org/mciap/FieldGuide.pdf.

Maine Chapter of the International Appalachian Trail. 2018. "2018 Maine IAT Trail Guide." *Maine International Appalachian Trail.* June 26. https://docs.wixstatic.com/ugd/56fce5_fcce9588eb5f478da469cb8479e98952.pdf.

Maine Department of Conservation and National Park Service. 1982. "Maine Rivers Study." https://www.maine.gov/dep/gis/datamaps/lawb_maine_river_survey/pdf/1982MaineRiversStudy_FinalReport2011.pdf.

Maine Department of Inland Fisheries and Game, "First Report of the Commissioners of Fisheries of the State of Maine, 1867" (1868). *Inland Fisheries and Wildlife Documents. 24.* https://digitalmaine.com/ifw_docs/24.

Maine Department of Inland Fisheries and Wildlife. 2019. "Mammals." https://www.maine.gov/ifw/fish-wildlife/wildlife/species-information/mammals/index.html.

Maine Department of Inland Fisheries and Wildlife. 2017. "Wildlife Division Research & Management Report 2017." https://www.maine. gov/ifw/docs/2017%20Research%20and%20Management%20Report_ FINAL_9-5-17.pdf.

Maine Forest Service. 2008. "Forest Trees of Maine." *Maine Department of Conservation.* https://www.maine.gov/dacf/mfs/publications/ handbooks_guides/forest_trees/.

Maine Geological Survey. 2005. "Surficial Geologic History of Maine." *Department of Agriculture, Conservation and Forestry.* https://www.maine. gov/dacf/mgs/explore/surficial/facts/surficial.htm.

Maine Woods Forever. 2013. "Thoreau–Wabanaki Trail: East Branch of the Penobscot River Map and Guide." Orono, ME: University of Maine Press.

Marvinney, Robert G. 2012. Sugarloaf Mountain near Shin Pond, Maine— A Classic Geological Locality: Maine Geological Survey, Geologic Facts and Localities, Circular GFL-182, 17 p. *Maine Geological Survey Publications.* 473. http://digitalmaine.com/mgs_publications/473.

National Park Service. 2019. "Katahdin Woods and Waters National Monument." *National Park Service.* https://www.nps.gov/kaww/index.htm.

Native Plant Trust. 2020. "Acorus americanus: Several-veined Sweetflag." *Go Botany.* https://gobotany.nativeplanttrust.org/species/acorus/americanus/.

Neff, John W. 2006. *Katahdin, An Historic Journey: Legends, Explorations, and Preservation of Maine's Highest Peak.* Boston, MA: Appalachian Mountain Club Books.

New Hampshire Fish and Game Department. 2019. "Fallfish (Semotilus corporalis)." *New Hampshire Fish and Game.* https://www.wildlife.state. nh.us/fishing/profiles/fallfish.html.

Northern Forest Canoe Trail. 2005. "NFCT Map 11, Maine: Moosehead/ Penobscot Region." Seattle, WA: The Mountaineers Books.

Northern Forest Canoe Trail. 2004. "NFCT Map 12, Maine: Allagash Region—South." Seattle, WA: The Mountaineers Books.

Potila, Jessica. 2016. "Allagash Celebrates 50th Anniversary of Wilderness Waterway." *Fiddlehead Focus.* August 24. https:// fiddleheadfocus.com/2016/08/24/news/community/top-stories/ allagash-celebrates-50th-anniversary-of-wilderness-waterway/.

Smith, Edmund Ware. 1958. *A Treasury of the Maine Woods.* Camden, ME: Down East Magazine.

Smith, Edmund Ware. 1965. *Upriver and Down: Stories from the Maine Woods.* New York, NY: Holt, Rinehart, and Winston.

Smith, George. 2016. *Maine Sporting Camps*. Camden, ME: Down East Books.

Steenstra, E. Peter. 2014. "Charles Atkins—A Pioneer in Fisheries Conservation." *US Fish and Wildlife Service Northeast Region.* November 17. https://usfwsnortheast.wordpress.com/2014/11/17/charles-atkins-a-pioneer-in-fisheries-conservation/.

Stolte, Lawrence. 1981. *The Forgotten Salmon of the Merrimack*. Department of the Interior, Northeast Region.

Thoreau, Henry David. 2006. *The Maine Woods*. Stilwell, KS: Digireads.com Publishing.

US Department of the Interior. 2017. "Interior Department Releases List of Monuments under Review, Announces First-ever Formal Public Comment Period for Antiquities Act Monuments." *US Department of the Interior.* May 5. https://www.doi.gov/pressreleases/interior-department-releases-list-monuments-under-review-announces-first-ever-formal.

US Fish and Wildlife Service. 2019. "White-Nose Syndrome Response Team." https://www.whitenosesyndrome.org/.

Werler, Ed. 2003. *The Call of Katahdin: Life in Werler's Woods*. Yarmouth, ME: Cranberry Knoll Publishers LLC.

Whippie, Johnson. 2018. *Maverick and Goose Go for a Paddle: Webster Brook and the East Branch of the Penobscot*. Unpublished.

CAMPING AND MILEAGE STATISTICS

Date	Evening camp	Day's miles	Total miles
July 8	Wassataquoik campsite, KAWW	5.7	5.7
July 9	Lunksoos campsite, KAWW	7.7	13.4
July 10	Grand Pitch campsite, KAWW	11.0	24.4
July 11	Matagamon Wilderness Campground	10.0	34.4
July 16	"E" Ledge, West Br. Penobscot River	14.5	48.9
July 17	Shallow Bay campsite, Lobster Lake	15.8	64.7
July 18	Big Ragmuff campsite, West Br. Penobscot River	12.3	77.0
July 19	Canvas Dam campsite, Caucomgomoc Stream	17.1	94.1
July 20	Caucomgomoc Dam campsite, Caucomgomoc Lake	10.6	104.7
July 21	Ice Cave campsite, Allagash Lake	11.7	116.4
July 22	Little Allagash Falls campsite, Allagash Stream	7.5	123.9
July 23	Lost Spring campsite, Chamberlain Lake	5.7	129.6
July 24	Boy Scout campsite, Chamberlain Lake	13.7	143.3
July 25	Murphy's Field campsite, Telos Lake	6.7	150.0
July 26	Webster Outlet lean-to, Webster Lake	8.5	158.5
July 27	Little East campsite, Webster Stream	10.2	168.7
July 28	Matagamon Wilderness Campground	13.3	182.0
July 29	Pond Pitch campsite, East Br. Penobscot River, KAWW	8.4	190.4
July 30	Big Seboeis campsite, East Br. Penobscot River, KAWW	11.8	202.2
July 31	Brown Island, East Br. Penobscot River	11.0	213.2
August 1	Home	6.8	220.0

ABOUT THE AUTHOR

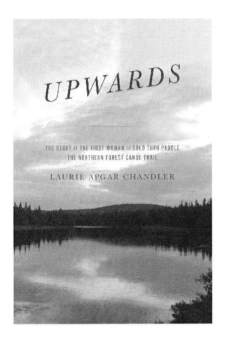

When life took a dramatic turn over a decade ago, it was a moment of awakening for Laurie Apgar Chandler. Her first expedition, a solo kayak trip across Maine that she called "Paddle for Hope," raised more than $10,000 for the Maine Children's Cancer Program. Four years later, at age 53, Chandler became the first woman to solo thru-paddle the 740-mile Northern Forest Canoe Trail, a story chronicled in her inspirational debut memoir. *Upwards: The Story of the First Woman to Solo Thru-Paddle the Northern Forest Canoe Trail* (2017) is available on the author's website (laurieachandler.com), at a host of amazing independent bookstores and outdoor suppliers, and from Maine Authors Publishing (www.maineauthorspublishing.com).